GOOD FISHING

IN THE ADIRONDACKS

GOOD FISHING

IN THE ADIRONDACKS

from Lake Champlain to the Streams of Tug Hill

Dennis Aprill

Second Edition, Revised

Backcountry Publications
Woodstock, Vermont

An Invitation to the Reader
With time, access points may change and road numbers, signs, and landmarks referred to in this book may be altered. If you find that such changes have occurred near the waters described in this book, please let the author and publisher know, so that corrections may be made in future editions. Other comments and suggestions are also welcome. Address all correspondence to:

Fishing Editor
The Countryman Press
PO Box 748
Woodstock, Vermont 05091

©1992, 1999 The Countryman Press
Second edition, revised and expanded
Originally published: Tarrytown, N.Y.: Northeast Sportsman's
Press, 1990

Library of Congress Cataloging in Publication Data
Good Fishing in the Adirondacks : from Lake Champlain to
the streams of Tug Hill / Dennis Aprill, editor. — 2nd ed.
p. cm.
Includes index.
ISBN-10: 0-88150-452-1
ISBN-13: 978-0-88150-452-1
1. Fishing—New York (State)—Adirondack Mountains
Region. 2. Fishing—New York (State)—Adirondack Mountains Region—Guidebooks. 3. Adirondack Mountains
(N.Y.)—Guidebooks I. Aprill, Dennis
SH529.G66 1999
799.1'1'097475—dc21   98-52993
                                              CIP

Maps created by Larry Boutis and drawn by Jim Capossela.
Map corrections for the second edition and new maps
by Jacques Chazaud.

Published by Backcountry Publications
A division of The Countryman Press, PO Box 748,
Woodstock, Vermont 05091

Distributed by W. W. Norton & Company, Inc.
500 Fifth Avenue, New York, New York 10110
Printed in the United States of America
10 9 8 7 6 5 4

ACKNOWLEDGMENTS

Because of the large number of authors involved with this book, it is not possible to list all of the dozens of people who helped with its preparation. The publisher would therefore like to offer a blanket thank-you to all those kind individuals, and to add a special thanks to the helpful people in the Adirondack offices of the New York State Department of Environmental Conservation, especially Walt Kretzer of the Adirondack Lake Survey Corporation for his help with the acid rain section.

Credit must also be given to the photographers whose work added greatly to the project. They are: Dennis Aprill, Allen Benas, Jim Capossela, Peter Casamento, Joe Hackett, Ron Kolodziej, New York State Department of Environmental Conservation, *Plattsburgh Press-Republican*, Marty Rosencrantz, Alice Vera, Robert Zajac, and Tony C. Zappia, and for the cover photo, Nancie Battaglia.

© 1999 The Countryman Press

N

CANADA

VT

NY

NH

401

LAKE ONTARIO

81

MA

90

90

88

17

87

CT

PA

17

84

95

84

80

80

NJ

ATLANTIC
OCEAN

81

95

401

15

0   100   200 miles

CONTENTS

List of Maps 9
Preface to the Second Edition 11
About the Editor 12

INTRODUCTION 13

CHAPTER ONE 19
Lake Champlain: Cool-Water Species
Bernie Jandreau

CHAPTER TWO 33
Lake Champlain: Cold-Water Species
Peter Casamento

CHAPTER THREE 47
Salmon Fever!
Ken Coleman, with Jim Hotaling

CHAPTER FOUR 57
The Mighty Saranac
John Spissinger

CHAPTER FIVE 71
The Legendary Ausable
Francis Betters

CHAPTER SIX 87
In the Heart of the Adirondacks
Brian McDonnell

CHAPTER SEVEN 97
Backcountry Fishing Trips
Dennis Aprill

CHAPTER EIGHT 107
The Peaceful Schroon Lake Area
Val De Cesare, updated by Val De Cesare, his son

CHAPTER NINE 121
Lake George
Robert Zajac, with Ricky Doyle

CHAPTER TEN 133
The Beautiful Tahawus Region
Robert Zajac

CHAPTER ELEVEN 145
Washington and Saratoga Counties:
Fishing the Eastern Slopes
Tracy Lamanec

CHAPTER TWELVE...155
Exciting Fishing Just North of the Thruway
Ron Kolodziej

CHAPTER THIRTEEN 165
The Great Southwestern Wilderness
Don Williams

CHAPTER FOURTEEN 177
The Secret Streams of Tug Hill
Allen Benas

CHAPTER FIFTEEN 185
Back in Time on the Oswegatchie
Peter O'Shea

CHAPTER SIXTEEN 199
The Raquette River: Highway through the Mountains
Tony C. Zappia

CHAPTER SEVENTEEN 211
Fishing Pole, Paddle, and Portage
Joe Hackett

CHAPTER EIGHTEEN 223
The St. Lawrence River
Allen Benas

LIST OF MAPS

Fig. 1.1 Lake Champlain, South 20
Fig. 2.1 Lake Champlain, North 34
Fig. 3.1 The Boquet River 46
Fig. 3.2 Lower Ausable River 53
Fig. 4.1 Saranac River, Main Stem 58
Fig. 4.2 Saranac River—Plattsburg 68
Fig. 5.1 Ausable River, Upper West Branch 72
Fig. 5.2 Ausable River, Lower West Branch 77
Fig. 5.3 Ausable River, East Branch 83
Fig. 6.1 Central Lakes Area 88
Fig. 6.2 Upper Saranac Lake 95
Fig. 7.1 Northville Lake Placid Trail 98
Fig. 8.1 South Schroon River 108
Fig. 8.2 Schroon Lake 115
Fig. 9.1 Lake George, North 122
Fig. 9.2 Lake George, South 125
Fig. 10.1 Upper Hudson Region 132
Fig. 11.1 The Battenkill 144
Fig. 11.2 Lakes Cossayuna and Lauderdale 147
Fig. 11.3 Saratoga Lake 150
Fig. 12.1 West Canada Creek Trophy Section 154
Fig. 13.1 Limekiln Lake 164
Fig. 13.2 The Fulton Chain 168
Fig. 14.1 Tug Hill 176
Fig. 15.1 Cranberry Lake 186
Fig. 15.2 Oswegatchie River 189
Fig. 16.1 Raquette and Forked Lakes 198
Fig. 16.2 Carry Falls Reservoir 207
Fig. 17.1 St. Regis Canoe Area 210
Fig. 17.2 Bog River Canoe Area 218

Map Legend

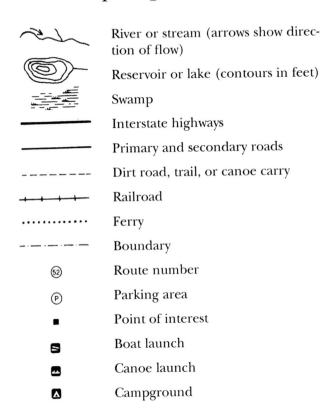

River or stream (arrows show direction of flow)

Reservoir or lake (contours in feet)

Swamp

Interstate highways

Primary and secondary roads

Dirt road, trail, or canoe carry

Railroad

Ferry

Boundary

Route number

Parking area

Point of interest

Boat launch

Canoe launch

Campground

PREFACE TO THE SECOND EDITION

It's been nine years since *Good Fishing in the Adirondacks* came out, and there have been many changes since then. These changes are reflected in this new, expanded edition. Within the chapters on Lake Champlain, Lake George, the Ausable and Saranac Rivers, the St. Lawrence Seaway, and many Adirondack waters in between, we've included the latest information about fish ladders, lamprey control programs, fish stocking, fishing techniques and regulations, as well as new suggestions for fishing in the backcountry, finding landlocked salmon, and discovering other highlights of the region.

–Dennis Aprill

ABOUT THE EDITOR

Dennis Aprill is a licensed New York State guide (#1474) and member of the New York State Outdoor Guides Association. He has fished extensively in northern New York and Canada. He is also the outdoors columnist for the *Plattsburgh Press-Republican* and a frequent contributor to *Adirondack Life* magazine. Books he has authored are *Paths Less Traveled*, an Adirondack hiking guide, and *Mammals of the Adirondacks* (coauthor). When not fishing and writing, Dennis teaches English and journalism classes at the State University of New York, Plattsburgh. He lives with his wife and two children in a remote section of the eastern Adirondacks.

Introduction

Imagine for a moment that you are suspended 30,000 feet directly above Mount Marcy, New York State's highest mountain. The high peaks appear as a somewhat off-center hub of a gigantic wheel with rivers radiating like spokes toward every point on the compass. Flowing north you would see the Raquette and St. Regis; to the east the Saranac, Ausable, and Boquet; to the south the Schroon and the Hudson; and to the west the Moose and the Beaver. From this preferred vantage point, not only would you start to get an idea of the immensity and wildness of the region, but a peculiar geological truth might sneak into your consciousness: The Adirondacks are a large dome eroded away (though certainly not uniformly) in every direction by flowing water.

If the day were especially clear, you might even be treated to the sight of two gigantic lakes to the east and south; to a spider web of streams laced across an elevated land mass to the southwest; to a huge river to the northwest. Lake George, Lake Champlain, Tug Hill, the St. Lawrence River—all these tempting possibilities might come into view. And then another reality would hit home: There is an awful lot of water just outside the Adirondacks—in all directions, as a matter of fact.

This book, then, is about fishing in northern New York, roughly that area north of the New York Thruway. It focuses not only on the wild and beautiful central Adirondacks, but also on the vast water systems on the fringes. Through the voices of local writers, all of whom live in northern New York and many of whom were born here, this book takes you to remote brook trout ponds and intimate streams. It leads you to larger blue-ribbon fly-fishing rivers. It guides you to crystalline lakes where swim lake trout, salmon, bass, muskies, pike, and much more.

With a culture and a history both unique and varied, this great wilderness of the east has been consecrated by artists in every possible medium: photography, painting, poetry, mountain crafts, and, of course, writing. It is still a beautiful, lightly settled region—only 120,000 people live full time within the Adirondack Blue Line—and it's so inspiring that a modern-day angler might yet share the sentiments of W.H.H. "Adirondack" Murray, who described in *Adventures in the Wilderness* the first morning of an Adirondack fishing adventure more than a century ago: "How cool the water; how fresh the air; how clear the sky; how fragrant the breath of balsam and pine; O luxury of luxuries, to have a lake of crystal water for your wash bowl, the morning zephyr for a towel, the whitest sand for soap and the odor of aromatic trees for perfumes! What belle or millionaire can boast of such surroundings?"

We hope this book will show you some of the vast potential and astonishing diversity of fishing in the Adirondack region and will lead you to many enjoyable adventures. If you have suggestions, comments, or corrections for future editions of the guide, please write to Dennis Aprill, ℅ The Countryman Press, PO Box 748, Woodstock, VT 05091.

A NOTE ON THE MAPS

Because of the limiting size of a book page and the scale of the area being drawn, only very select points of interest are depicted on the maps in this book. We have not been able to show all secondary roads or access trails. Please use an atlas for navigation when driving to the lakes and rivers, and use these maps to better understand the text and provide a starting point for trip planning.

SOME FACTS ABOUT ACID RAIN

One of the most immense environmental problems of our age is acid rain, also called acid deposition. The Adirondacks is one of the areas of North America that has been hardest hit by this insidious menace, and the publicity has led many anglers to believe that most Adirondack waters are "dead." This is far from the case, since good fishing still abounds in stream and pond, lake and river. Yet it is true that about 200 high-elevation ponds here have been wiped out by acid rain and that about 300 more are threatened. In addition, certain headwater tributary streams have been affected to the point at which fish life has been greatly diminished or even eradicated.

Acid rain stems from the chemical reaction of sulfur and nitrogen oxides with water in the atmosphere. These chemicals are primarily released into the atmosphere via the smokestacks of factories and the tailpipes of motorized vehicles. Basic high school chemistry demonstrates that when you combine the oxides of these chemicals with H_2O, you get H_2SO_4 and HNO_3, or sulfuric acid and nitric acid. Here in the late 20th century it is literally raining (and snowing) acid. Not only has this hurt aquatic life, but it is now starting to slowly kill some of our higher elevation forests. It is safe to assume that as acid rain worsens—and the woeful "wait and see" attitude of the federal government has assured that it will—its direct impact on human health will be exacerbated.

The relative acidity or alkalinity of any solution depends on its concentration of hydrogen ions. It is expressed as a number on a logarithmic scale ranging from 0 to 14.0. A pH of 7.0 is neutral. A change of one pH unit, for example from 6.0 to 5.0, indicates a tenfold increase in hydrogen ion concentration. Normal rain water is 5.6. The pH of acid rain is lower. How much lower determines the magnitude of the threat. In the mid-1970s, the mean pH of 214 high-elevation Adirondack ponds was about 4.75. Some species can tolerate (at least in the short term) this degree of acidity, but most cannot. Anything below 5.0 is generally bad news.

And that leads us to the classifications used in dealing with acid rain. Waters having a pH of 6.0 or higher are considered "satisfactory." Those between 5.0 and 6.0 are considered "endangered." Those below 5.0 are termed "critical."

In a synoptic chemistry survey that took place between 1975 and 1982, 1,047 Adirondack lakes and ponds were sampled. This is about 38 percent of the 2,759 ponded waters located within the region (transitory beaver and bog ponds would push that 2,759 figure higher). All the sampled waters fell within a modified 1,000-foot elevation perimeter, which roughly coincides with the Adirondack Park boundary. Approximately 92 percent of the estimated 246,271 acres of ponded water within the zone were sampled. The results were as follows:

Waters	(%)	Classification	Acres	(%)
199	(19.0)	Critical (below 5.0 pH)	8,796	(3.9)
264	(25.2)	Endangered (5.0–6.0 pH)	23,346	(10.3)
584	(55.8)	Satisfactory (above 6.0 pH)	193,710	(85.8)

Surveys done by the Adirondack Lake Survey Corporation covered 1,469 ponds or lakes. Of these, 1,123 contained fish and 346 were without fish. In looking at these two surveys, though, it should be remembered that some of the now fishless ponds undoubtedly never did contain fish.

In spite of that qualifier, there is no denying that acid rain has either wiped out or reduced the fishing opportunity on about 25 percent of fishable Adirondack ponds. The surveys have shown that ponds smaller than 20 acres and at elevations greater than 2,000 feet are at greatest risk. Though less studied at this point, certain smaller streams at higher elevations have also been seriously affected. Taking a region-wide look, we see that waters in the southwestern Adirondacks have been hardest hit. This is partially because of higher precipitation levels in this part of the Adirondacks. As an example, many ponds and lakes just north of Stillwater Reservoir, including ones in the scenic Five Ponds Area, have been strongly affected.

Backpacking in for native brook trout is an old Adirondack tradition and is well covered in this book. Yet it is clear from the preceding discussion that an angler heading out into the brush by foot or by canoe should find out which ponds to avoid. Here, the New York State Department of Environmental Conservation (DEC) can help.

Regional DEC offices in Ray Brook, Warrensburg, and Watertown (for location see the resources) can provide specific information on most waters within their jurisdiction for which current survey data exists. Other information, including scientific reports on acid precipitation, can be obtained by writing to the Adirondack Lake Survey Corporation, Ray Brook, NY 12977.

A NOTE OF CAUTION

As if acid rain weren't enough of a threat to our largest wilderness area, you should know that the New York State Department of Health warns that many fish in New York waters contain certain potentially harmful contaminants. This is not true of many areas of the Adirondacks, but nevertheless you are advised to consult the New York State DEC for further details before eating any fish you may catch. Many of the current advisories will be seen on the inside of the front cover of the DEC annual publication *New York State Fishing Regulations Guide.*

Colin Aprill, at age seven, with a lake trout.

CHAPTER ONE

Lake Champlain: Cool-Water Species

BERNIE JANDREAU

Grandly situated between the majestic Adirondack Mountains and the Green Mountains of Vermont lies beautiful Lake Champlain. At any midlake vantage point, one is treated to an awesome panoramic display of lofty peaks flowing down to lush green valleys bordering on the edge of shimmering blue.

Often called a great lake (being the sixth-largest freshwater lake in America, behind only the Great Lakes), Champlain boasts 585 miles of shoreline, 435 square miles of water, and 110 miles of length from its southern terminus at Whitehall, New York, to its outlet at the Richelieu River just north of the Canadian border. Its maximum depth of 401 feet can be found at the lake's widest point between Port Kent, New York, and Burlington, Vermont—a distance of 11 miles.

Many islands dot the surface of Lake Champlain, some of them huge and some of them very small. A host of them are rookeries for various species of wild birds, especially the Four Brothers Islands just south of Willsboro Point. Seagulls, great blue herons, and cormorants are nesting guests here, and mid-April through May can be a birdwatcher's paradise.

As one might guess, the prospect of water sports is as inviting to many as is the beautiful scenery. Sail- and powerboats are

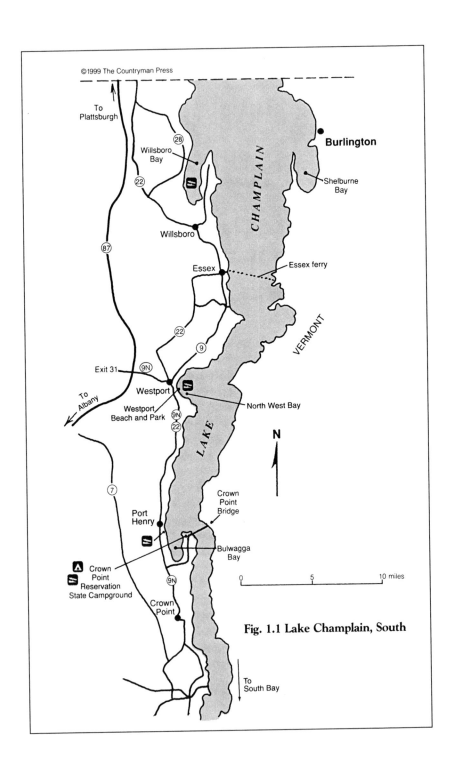

To
Plattsburgh

28

Willsboro
Bay

22

Willsboro

87

Essex — Essex ferry

CHAMPLAIN

Burlington

Shelburne
Bay

VERMONT

22

9

Exit 31

9N

To
Albany

Westport

Westport
Beach and Park

9N

22

North West Bay

LAKE

N

7

Port
Henry

Crown
Point
Bridge

Bulwagga
Bay

Crown
Point
Reservation
State Campground

9N

0   5   10 miles

Crown
Point

Fig. 1.1 Lake Champlain, South

To
South Bay

seldom in short supply on the lake, but with a body of water this size, they are usually of little concern to the angler. An imaginary line separating the states of New York and Vermont extends the entire length of the lake. As there is no reciprocal agreement between the two regarding fishing rights—although there may be soon—it is wise to buy a Vermont fishing license if you plan to spend any time here. Lacking that, purchase lake charts that show the boundaries. The lake is very narrow at both the north and south ends, and one could easily venture into the other state's waters without realizing it.

FISHING ON LAKE CHAMPLAIN

In this chapter we will be dealing exclusively with the cool-water species of Lake Champlain (the cold-water species are discussed in chapter 2). Our discussion will take us up the western shore of Champlain from Ticonderoga, New York, all the way to the Canadian border—a distance of about 100 miles. For your fishing information, I will name several tributaries as well as launch ramps, shore-fishing sites, and nearby towns and villages for supplies and accommodations.

Before we start our trip, a word of caution: If you plan to fish the lake from a boat, be sure to have proper working safety equipment. My 60 years of experience on this lake have taught me many lessons. A peaceful, sleeping beauty can suddenly turn into a raging witch. Carry items like a weather radio, flare kit, life jackets, fire extinguisher, anchor, oars, rain gear, and an auxiliary motor if you have one. And by all means, the larger the boat the better. I am not implying that the lake is always treacherous. I'm merely pointing out that it can get rough out there, especially in the summer when sudden storms out of the west are down on you before you've had a chance to take cover. There are more calm, relatively placid days than bad ones, though.

Your fishing opportunities on Lake Champlain are superb. With some 23 cool-water species, you have the kind of variety that is found in very few other waters in the northeast. In this chapter we will deal mainly with the most popular species: black bass, northern pike, walleyed pike, pickerel, muskellunge, and certain of the more popular panfish.

TICONDEROGA AND VICINITY

At the village of Ticonderoga, look for the signs directing you to the ferry to Vermont. You'll find the state boat landing adjacent to the ferry landing. The ramp is good, with plenty of parking. The village of "Ti" can take care of all your boating and fishing needs, as well as food and lodging. Historic Fort Ticonderoga overlooks the lake and is a must-see attraction. All this is just minutes from the ramp.

Some excellent fishing for bass, both largemouth and smallmouth, can be found in the vicinity. As this end of the lake is narrow and shallow, you will find lots of weed beds and lily pads, with the result that the largemouth predominates. Live minnows, spinnerbaits, surface lures, and rubber worms will work best for you here.

Northern pike, pickerel, walleyes, perch, crappies, and sunfish are also found throughout this area. The same lures mentioned above will take the pike and pickerel, and some panfish. Trolled night crawlers or minnows are good for the walleyes, while a can of garden worms is still best for the little fellows.

The best time to fish this area is from mid-May through mid-October, although the ice fishing is excellent all winter. As a general rule, boat fishing is always the best way to cover the most water, even though some limited bank fishing is available.

PORT HENRY AND BULWAGGA BAY

Moving north we enter the village of Port Henry. An excellent, well-maintained state launch ramp is located right in the heart of town. All facilities are at your fingertips. Five miles in either direction (north or south) from the launch ramp will provide you with plenty of good fishing for all species mentioned above. In addition, cold-water fish such as lake trout, landlocked salmon, and a stray steelhead now and then will turn up. Ice fishing for smelt is excellent here.

Looking southeast to south from the launch ramp, you will see the Crown Point Bridge and Bulwagga Bay, two excellent fishing areas. The bridge abutments hold some fine smallmouths, while in the deeper water under this span trolling will often produce walleyes.

Bob Morrison, and noted Lake Champlain guide and author, Don McKee, try for largemouth on expansive Bulawagga Bay. This bay, plus the nearby Crown Point Bridge, are two Champlain hot spots.

Adjacent to the bridge on the southwest side is the Crown Point Reservation State Park and Campground, a nicely maintained scenic facility overlooking the lake. A T-shaped covered pier here extends a few hundred feet into the lake and is a good spot to catch some panfish and an occasional bass or pike. A small launch ramp is located about 100 yards from the pier and is available to anyone using the park. A small park entrance fee is charged.

Bulwagga Bay is just ¼ mile west of the bridge and is a haven for largemouth bass, pike, and pickerel. Panfishing in this bay is great for perch, crappie, sunfish, and bluegill. The bay is easily identified as it adjoins the main highway (Route 22 North) into Port Henry and the launch ramp.

As you enter the bay you will see a large section of riprap on the right side. Smallmouths and an occasional largemouth will be holding on these rocks. The entire perimeter of the bay becomes grassed over by midsummer with an open channel down the middle. Pike, pickerel, and largemouth will be holding in or near this grass.

On the left side, you will see a short peninsula of rocks jutting out toward the center of the bay and marked by warning buoys. Don't pass up this area. The south side drops off into 15–20 feet of water at the end, and the bottom works gradually up to the main shoreline. Weed beds abound just off these rocks, and a variety of fish, especially largemouths, are abundant. Rubber worms and spinnerbaits have filled my live well many times here.

To get the most out of Bulwagga Bay, try to get there in May, June, or July. If your fishing trips involve camping, an excellent campground is on the shore at the entrance to the bay. The lake starts to deepen north of Port Henry, so concentrate efforts on Bulwagga Bay, the Crown Point Bridge, and south. Weedy coves and rocky ledges are the rule south of the bridge. Add some crankbaits and jigs to your arsenal of lures for the smallmouths hanging around the rock piles and points in this section. Spinnerbaits and rubber worms will pull the largemouths and pike out of the weed beds. Best time to fish this general area? Spring through fall.

WESTPORT AND NORTH TO PLATTSBURGH

I won't dwell long on this section, because it will be covered in chapter 2. However, some good smallmouth fishing can be found along the rocky shoreline that abounds in the area. Steep cliffs jut down to rocky points all the way south to Port Henry and north to Split Rock Point at Whallon Bay. Summer and fall fishing is best, and a boat is almost mandatory. The launch is located in the village, and services are limited to a few restaurants and marinas. Some accommodations are available.

Approximately 4 miles north of the village of Keeseville flows one of the lake's major tributaries, the Ausable River. During midsummer, low water makes the lower section (Route 9 bridge to mouth) barely fishable. However, spring fishing—mid-April through mid-June—is excellent for salmon and smallmouth bass. The Ausable and other key Champlain tributaries are discussed at length in other chapters.

Just south of the city of Plattsburgh is the Valcour Island area. This section is prime water for walleyes, smallmouths, and some real big pike. The state launch ramp is conveniently located off Route 9 directly across from the island and has excellent parking and restroom facilities. Several marinas, motels, and restaurants are located within yards of the ramp. The island itself is a haven for boaters, not only because it provides shelter during sudden storms but also because of its scenic beauty and sandy beaches. A "primitive" campground (limited facilities) maintained by the state is on the northwest side and is, of course, only accessible by boat.

Valcour's rocky shoreline makes for some good smallmouth bass fishing, and deep-water trolling around the island can produce some really big pike. A surprise bonus may also turn up in the form of a big lake trout, a nice salmon, or a chunky brown trout.

Most significant in this area is the good walleyed pike fishing. Approximately ¾ mile north of Valcour Island is Crab Island. Much smaller than Valcour, it provides the necessary line of sight between the islands to place you over the reefs for the best walleye fishing. As walleyes are predominantly night feeders, this kind of fishing is always best after dark. The fish rise at this time from the bottom to feed on bait fish on or near the surface. Lures trolled with small split shot produce well.

In the last few years, planer board trolling has really taken off and has proven itself to be an effective night-fishing tool.

Fishing these same reefs during daylight will give you some action, but you will have to go deep. Bait walker sinkers or three-way swivel rigs will get you down to the big ones. Perch school up after spawning and move out into the main lake. The bottom structure around Valcour Island is basically rocky with some sandy or pebbly beaches scattered here and there. Locate the school with your depth finder, or simply cast to the shoreline as you move around the island. My favorite bait for schooling perch is the Mister Twister Sassy Shad in shad color mounted on a ⅛-ounce jighead. The inch-and-a-half size seems to work best, and six-pound test performs well with this setup. You can either swim the lure or jig it. Of course, small minnows and the old reliable garden worm work well also.

THE SARANAC RIVER

Flowing through the city of Plattsburgh, the Saranac River has fine spring fishing for salmon, walleye, and smallmouth bass. The best time to fish it is mid-April to early June. The salmon arrive first, followed by the walleyes and bass. Like the Ausable, the water recedes in June, so the fish move out early.

All of the fishing is concentrated at the mouth of the river and several hundred yards upstream. Beyond this the river becomes too shallow to navigate, and a dam 2 miles upstream stops all fish progress. Bank fishing is popular here. The city of Plattsburgh offers all services, of course.

If you are fortunate enough to be in this area during the perch spawning season—usually April through the first or second week of May—you're in for a real treat.

Just north of the Saranac River is Cumberland Bay. Starting at the Plattsburgh City Beach and running east 2 miles to Cumberland Head Point is some of the best spring perch fishing you will find anywhere in the lake. The bottom is rocky and ideal for spawning perch. Huge schools move in here, and the action can be fantastic. The same methods I mentioned earlier will work well; just bring along some good-sized coolers because you're going to pick up lots of "slabs."

POINT AU ROCHE, LITTLE CHAZY RIVER, AND ROUSES POINT

The next three fishing areas are my favorite—and the most important—on the western shore of Lake Champlain. Each abounds with cool-water species. Our fishing areas in this section will extend 2½ miles south to Treadwell Bay and 6 miles north to the Little Chazy River. We will be covering various types of fish-holding structure along the way.

Point Au Roche

Approximately 4 miles north of Plattsburgh on Route 9, you will find signs directing you to the old Point Au Roche boat ramp. The ramp is well maintained and has ample parking and portable johns. Limited lodging and other facilities are available.

As you look to the northeast from the ramp, you will see Isle La Motte (named after the French captain Sieur de la Motte, who commanded the fort built on the island in 1666). This island sits in Vermont waters.

Moving south out of the launch ramp, you will notice the rocky shoreline almost immediately. This structure continues all the way down to Long Point at Treadwell Bay. Smallmouth bass relate to this structure, so start fishing the shoreline 300 yards or so from the ramp. Before you venture too far, turn around and notice two red buoys directly behind you. The northernmost buoy marks a small rock pile and almost always has some smallmouths hanging around. The southern buoy marks La-Roche Reef and is excellent structure for walleyes.

Back on the shoreline, cover all the good-looking points on your way down to Long Point. The point itself extends underwater almost ¾ mile due south to a red buoy that is visible from the point. Smallmouths will be on top of this structure, and walleyes will be stacked somewhere on the sharp drop-off on the east side of the point all the way out to the buoy.

On the inside of Long Point, you will find Deep Bay, Middle Bay, and Short Point. Fish all around these points and bays for smallmouth and northern pike. The land in this area is state owned, and a new state park recently opened with a very nice boat launch and parking area with restrooms. The ramp is in

Middle Bay and is protected to all but a south wind. A small fee is charged to use the park and ramp. If you decide to launch here, you will see the park sign as you proceed down the Point Au Roche Road from Route 9.

Now let's move north from the ramp. About a mile north is North Point, known locally as Dicksons Point. Fish the point around into Monty Bay. The point is smallmouth country, and the bay is northern pike, pickerel, and largemouth bass territory. The south side of this bay is all weed beds and marsh grass. Check this area out carefully.

Little Chazy River

Starting at Wool Point on the north side of Monty Bay, work your way to the Little Chazy River. Cover all the rocky points for smallmouths and the many bays for pike and pickerel. The Little Chazy River is exceptionally good for largemouth bass in early spring. About June 15 the river becomes choked with weeds and is impassable by boat. The weedy section at the mouth of the river is fishable most of the season.

Another favorite area of mine is the Great Chazy River and the King's Bay section of the lake. Here, again, there is only limited lodging and other services. At the mouth of the Great Chazy you will find an excellent launching ramp maintained by the state. With room enough for 50 cars and trailers, it provides a good jumping-off point, not only for King's Bay but for all the good fishing areas both north and south of the river. The Canadian border is only 5 miles up the lake from this point.

The Great Chazy is a spring hot spot and is one of the few tributaries that harbor big muskies. Winding its way 4 miles up to the village of Champlain (there is a barrier at this point), the river provides good fishing for walleyes, bass, muskies, pike, pickerel, and hordes of panfish. Several bank areas are open to panfishing, and the peak time overall will be mid-April through early July. Muskie fishing is best in September and October.

The river flows into Lake Champlain at King's Bay, a large, shallow, weedy bay extending a ½ mile both north and south. One look at this bay is all you will need to picture the potential for bass and pike. Many species of panfish are also taken, both summer and winter. I know of no special hot spots in this bay; you can find fish over its entire length and breadth.

Rouses Point

And now last, but by no means least, is the Rouses Point section of Lake Champlain.

As launching ramps are virtually nonexistent in this area, I would recommend using the Chazy River Ramp. Several good fishing spots can be found all the way up to Rouses Point, a distance of about 5 miles.

After rounding Pont Au Fer and moving north from the Chazy, you will approach the first large weed bed at Catfish Bay. Pike, pickerel, largemouth bass, and several species of panfish frequent this area. The fishing is good here from early spring throughout the summer and into fall. There is little or no access for bank fishing.

Just to your north is the Rouses Point breakwater. A few quick casts at the very end will tell you if anybody's home. This breakwater is a good spot for those of you who don't own a boat, because it extends well out into the lake and always has good panfishing if the big boys aren't around. Accessibility by car is at the village limit south of town on Route 9N.

As you leave the breakwater, the village of Rouses Point will be spread out before you. The shoreline consists of weedy bays, rocky points, and several underwater rock-filled cribs. A lake chart would be very helpful here. However, a few days of observing other fishermen working this area will give you a pretty good idea of where the big ones are.

One outstanding feature you will encounter is the old railroad bridge crossing, an out-of-use span that runs over to Vermont. The bridge hasn't been used in 4 or 5 decades, since a fire destroyed a large section off the Vermont shore. But more than 7,000 wooden pilings are driven into the lake bottom here, creating some fantastic fish-holding structures. Big largemouths, smallmouths, northern pike, and many panfish species congregate here to feed on crayfish and the hordes of baitfish that flock to the protective shelter of the pilings.

Fish can be found in and around these pilings most of the

summer, but the best time is always early fall—September to mid-October. This is the time that the big "hawgs" start to feed heavily as they attempt to store up fat for the long winter ahead. Live minnows, crayfish, and frogs are great here, as are rubber worms and jig-and-pig combos. Other than these more or less weedless lures, your selection will be quite limited because of the hook-catching nature of the wooden pilings. The pilings extend from the New York shore to the Vermont shore with a break in the center for boat passage. That break is the dividing line separating the two states.

Slightly to the north of the old railroad bridge is the automobile bridge, opened in September 1987. The concrete pilings hold some smallmouths and pike as well as various panfish. Structure from the old torn-down bridge is only some 50–75 feet to the north, and this also holds some bass and pike.

The Canadian border is now less than ¼ mile away. On your left will be the ruins of old Fort Montgomery. The US border is just behind the fort. Good fishing for largemouth bass, northern pike, and pickerel will be found in the bays surrounding the fort. Trolling the center channel from the fort back south under the new bridge and on through the cut at the railroad bridge can produce some nice walleyes. Boat traffic will be a bit heavy here, especially on weekends. Try to schedule your trolling trips for weekdays.

The Rouses Point area has given me many pleasurable hours and some great fish. Although the village is relatively small, a few fine restaurants and good lodging are available.

In Lake Champlain, the fishing can be not only exceptional but extremely varied. When you consider the beautiful scenery and the many fascinating historic points on or near the lake, you have a fishing vacation package that can rival any in the country.

ABOUT THE AUTHOR

Bernie Jandreau is a native New Yorker born near the northern shore of Lake Champlain. Having actively fished Champlain since age 5, he has more than 60 years of experience on the lake. He was a fishing guide for 20 years, the last 12 years as head guide for the Adirondack-Champlain Guide Service in

Willsboro. Now retired, he spends his leisure time fishing, lec-
turing, and writing. He holds several bass-fishing titles and has
won more than 50 trophies.

FOOTNOTE: THE GREAT CHAZY RIVER

The Great Chazy River is often overlooked by anglers to the
south, but not by the increasing number of northern tier and
Canadian anglers who fish it annually. Its big draw is its diversity.
To illustrate this, let's start at the river's mouth.

From where the Great Chazy enters Lake Champlain upriver to the first dam, the fishing is excellent from ice-out until
the season closes. First there's bass, both large- and smallmouth.
The season begins in May. The best way to fish bass in this
section is by boat, either coming in from Lake Champlain or
launching at the Route 9B bridge.

Work the sections with downed trees or obvious underwater
structures using spinnerbaits or surface plugs. The mouth of
the river provides great perch fishing right after the ice goes
out, and there is, in addition, a large crappie population here.

Also along this stretch—from the mouth to the village of
Champlain—there are some very large muskellunge, some in
the 20-pound range. Years back a 32-pounder was taken out of
this section of river. For muskies, troll and cast near the weed
beds. Because muskies feed only once a week (when they gorge
themselves), some big fish will follow your line right up to the
boat without a hit, while others will readily take the first lure
they see. Try using top-water plugs like Jitterbugs, Crazy Crawlers, and large Rapalas.

The river's mouth is also a good place to catch some nice
walleyes. Troll using crawlers, floating jigheads, Green Mountain Grabbers, and Rapalas.

We're not done yet, because northern pike can also be
fished in the lower Great Chazy. Cast near the weed beds using
Daredevles and weedless spoons, like you would for muskie.

From Perry Mills to Mooers, the Great Chazy makes two
large U-shaped loops. This section is called the Oxbow. Here
you will find good muskie fishing. Use big shiners or other minnows with your rigs.

At Mooers Forks, the north branch joins the main stem of the Great Chazy; both are good brown trout streams, and both contain rainbows and native speckled trout. Because it flows through relatively open country, the north branch's water warms nicely during the summer, creating ideal conditions for brown trout. There is natural propagation of this species in both branches. Like elsewhere, go after browns using your favorite flies, spinnerbaits, or plugs.

Finally, let's look at Chazy Lake, the headwaters of the main branch of the Great Chazy. Just after ice-out, this lake is the place to go for lake trout as they feed near the surface. As the water warms, you will have to go to deep-trolling rigs. Chazy Lake, in addition, is excellent rainbow trout water; salmon can also be fished in this cold-water lake. There is a boat launch off Route 374.

Musky, northerns, panfish, walleyes, bass, trout of all kinds, and even salmon—the Great Chazy water system is truly a diverse fishery.

—Peter LaFountaine, Vice President of the Ridge Runners Sportsman's Club, Rouses Point

CHAPTER TWO

Lake Champlain: Cold-Water Species

PETER CASAMENTO

The preceding chapter offers much information on the impressive dimensions of Lake Champlain and its primary coolwater species. Well, this extraordinary body of water may be the ultimate two-story fishery. Let's now look at the stellar fishing that can be had here for cold-water species.

Lake Champlain probably has as many or more different types of catchable freshwater fish as any lake in the northeast. Landlocked salmon, lake trout, brown trout, rainbow trout, smelt, and whitefish are the main cold-water species, and these primarily inhabit the middle two-thirds of the lake. Lake trout and salmon are the most abundant of these gamefish. Hundreds of thousands of lakers and landlocks are stocked each year by New York and Vermont. In addition, fall salmon runs on some rivers have established some natural reproduction.

Lakers average 3–8 pounds, and a lot of lunkers weighing more than 10 pounds are caught. The salmon average 2–4 pounds, but mixed in are quite a few 6- to 8-pounders and an occasional trophy more than 10 pounds. Both rainbows (steelhead) and browns average 2–4 pounds with an occasional fish of 6–8 pounds.

The states of New York and Vermont began the Sea Lamprey Control Project on Lake Champlain, with the Ausable,

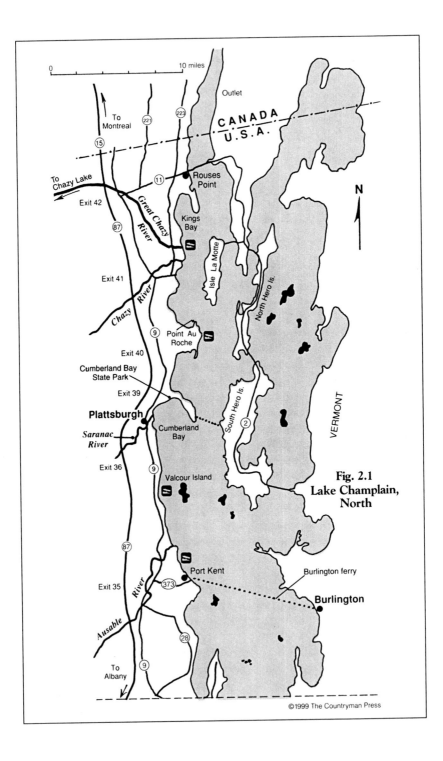

0   10 miles

Outlet

To
Montreal
221
223

CANADA
U.S.A.

15

To Chazy Lake

11   Rouses Point

Exit 42

87

Great Chazy River

Kings Bay

Isle La Motte

North Hero Is.

Exit 41

Chazy River

9   Point Au Roche

Exit 40

Cumberland Bay State Park

Exit 39

South Hero Is.

2

VERMONT

Plattsburgh

Saranac River

Cumberland Bay

Exit 36

9   Valcour Island

Fig. 2.1
Lake Champlain,
North

87

Port Kent

Burlington ferry

Exit 35

Ausable River

373

Burlington

28

9

To Albany

N

©1999 The Countryman Press

Saranac, and Boquet River deltas treated with lampricides in 1990 and 1991. Although thousands of cold-water gamefish already are caught and released each year, the average size of these fish continues to increase with lamprey control in place.

The most abundant cold-water species is smelt. Though not considered a gamefish, it is one of the most popular food fish among the natives. It is the main diet of cold-water gamefish. There are millions of smelt in Lake Champlain, and without them, there would not be much of a cold-water fishery. Smelt average 4–8 inches but occasionally grow to longer than 12 inches.

Whitefish inhabit the deep-water areas of the lake. Although they are not stocked, there are a lot of these fish in Lake Champlain. Until recently, whitefish were seldom caught, and most fishermen did not know they were even there. Fishing techniques used in other lakes across the country are now being used in Lake Champlain, and the whitefish is becoming a popular gamefish, as well as a popular food fish. Whitefish average 2–4 pounds and can reach a weight of 20 pounds.

SPRING

Ice-out on Lake Champlain is usually in late March or early April and, like clockwork, the day the ice goes out the salmon are in! This is the best time of the year for catching landlocked salmon in good numbers. These fish, along with browns and rainbows, concentrate in the mouths of the rivers and in or around the bays and points near the mouths of the rivers. This time of year the rivers are high from melting snows, washing lots of food down to the lake. The river temperatures are also quite a bit warmer than the lake temperature; this warmer water really attracts the fish. At this time of year, while the waters are high and murky, fishermen who troll or cast small bright spoons will be the most successful. For the live-bait fisherman, worms and night crawlers land the most fish.

About late April or early May, when the rains and melting snows have abated, the rivers and streams become crystal clear. This is the time for the lightest line and the smallest lures. Fly-casting streamers or trolling streamers with 2- to 4-pound-test line will catch the most fish. For the bait fisherman, live or dead smelt is best. The best river and stream mouth areas for the salmon and trout at this time of year are the Saranac, Ausable, Boquet, and Lachute Rivers and Putts Creek.

From ice-out until mid-May, lake trout and whitefish seem to be spread out in deep water. Fishermen using downriggers or lead core line are the most successful. Whitefish are caught on very small spoons and spinners, while the lake trout tend to hit on much larger spoons and Rapala-type lures.

From mid-May until late June, the landlocks, rainbows, browns, and whitefish are found near the surface over deep-water areas. The Point Au Roche to the Port Henry areas on the New York side are the most productive parts of the lake for these species. Trolling spoons either by flatlining or by the use of planer boards is most productive. Lake trout seem to be at all depths at this time of year, and a lot of trout are caught right close to shore in a couple of feet of water near rocky points. Many fishermen cast from shore or anchor their boats and cast to shore using ¼- to ¾-ounce jigs and spoons, while others use dead smelt fished just off the bottom. The most popular points for this shallow-water fishing are the Port Douglas to Port Kent area and the Willsboro Point to Westport areas in New York. Fishermen also enjoy success off the many islands and reefs in the lake at this time of year, especially Valcour Island, Schuyler Island, the Four Brothers Islands, Pumpkin Reef, Schuyler Reef, and Juniper and Diamond Islands.

SUMMER

About late June, as the surface temperature of the lake rises, the salmon, trout, whitefish, and smelt go deep. Downrigger trolling, trolling with lead core line, deep-water jigging, or fishing near the bottom with live or dead smelt are the only ways to catch these fish during the summer. Though fish can be graphed more than 200 feet down, most fish are caught 40–120 feet down. Many different sizes and types of flutter spoons, spinners, and minnow-imitating lures are used for deep-water trolling during the summer. The heavier spoons and bucktail jigs are used for jigging up lakers in deep water. During the hot

Fishing from shore on an early spring day.

The result!

summer months, finding the smelt grounds is the key to catching all the salmonids. Some of the major smelt areas are the deep-water areas off the mouths of the Ausable and Boquet Rivers, Willsboro Bay/Pumpkin Reef area, Schuyler Reef/Four Brothers Islands area, and the Whallon Bay to Westport area.

Next to winter ice fishing, this is the best time of year to catch smelt. Because most of the smelt are concentrated at different depths, jigging with small cut pieces of smelt is the most productive way to fill your bucket.

FALL

Fall is trophy time! Whether you dote on the cool-water species or the cold water, fall is the time for catching the biggest of what you're after.

About mid-September, when the air temperature drops below 70 degrees and the fall rains begin, the rivers and streams bring colder water down to Lake Champlain. The salmon, browns, and steelhead sense this and again swim upriver. At this time of year, these fish are not going up to feed, but to spawn. Even though the rivers and streams are high, Lake Champlain is about at its lowest level of the year. This means that the lake does not back the mouths of the rivers up as it does in the spring, so there is not enough water in the rivers for boat fishing. All of the fishing is done from the banks or by wading using streamers, flies, worms, or minnows. Most salmon that go upriver in the fall are 4 pounds or better.

Because these fish are on a spawning run, they are not feeding. Repeatedly casting or drifting a fly or bait by them is the only way to get them to strike, out of instinct or aggravation. All in all, the success ratio at this time of year is lower than in the spring even though the average size of the salmon caught is a lot bigger. Spawning continues through October and into early November. Afterward, most spent fish make their way back to the lake where they once again start to feed. The Boquet, Saranac, and Ausable Rivers are the very best fall bets for landlocks.

About mid-October, the surface temperature of Lake Champlain drops below 60 degrees, and once again there is great surface action for lake trout, whitefish, and the smaller browns, rainbows, and landlocks. In early November, the bigger trout and salmon, which have completed their spawning runs, once again are feeding and are more easily caught. Early November through December is the time to catch the biggest lakers. Mature lake trout, which are 6 pounds or better, move into the shallow water to spawn at this time. Most spawning takes place in less than 10 feet of water. Unlike the other trout and salmon, unless they are actually in the act of spawning, lakers will take lures and bait readily. As in the spring, casting ¼- to ¾-ounce spoons will get the big lakers in the shallow water. Trolling flutter spoons, flies, and minnow-type lures will take the most salmon, rainbows, browns, and the smaller lake trout. Fall is probably the best time to get a lot of whitefish, and the right ticket is small spoons, flies, and spinners. Once again, as in the spring, most of these fish are caught in shallow water or near the surface over deep water. This action extends right to ice-over, which could be anywhere from late December to mid-January.

WINTER

Most parts of Champlain are frozen over by late January. Ice fishing for smelt, lakers, and salmon first starts around the Ticonderoga to Port Henry area. This area is just south of the deep-water smelt grounds, where the bottom comes up to about 40 feet. Here the lake is much shallower and freezes over a lot sooner. As soon as the ice is safe enough, the local fishermen are out setting up their shanties. These shanties are mainly set up for smelt fishing. The fishermen jig through holes in the floor of the shanties using hand lines. At the end of the line are one or two single hooks tipped with pieces of cut smelt; above them is a 1-ounce or more pencil weight. This is the top method for catching smelt on Champlain.

With this method, some lake trout and salmon are taken incidentally. However, few local ice fishermen try for lakers and salmon. Lake Champlain is virtually untapped for this type of fishing. Tip-up fishing is probably the best way of getting lake trout and salmon in winter, and with state regulations allowing 15 tip-ups per person, a fisherman can cover a lot of territory. The best bait to use on the tip-ups is live or dead smelt fished from just under the ice to about 20 feet down. Jigging with special jigging Rapalas or with other types of ice jigs is the other way to take these fish.

A rare catch. Brian Doyle caught this 10-pound female muskellunge at the mouth of the Great Chazy River. Muskies are uncommon in Lake Champlain.

LURES, BAIT, AND TACKLE

The basic food fish for cold-water gamefish are smelt and yellow perch, so any lure or fly that represents these bait fish is a sensible choice. Daredevles, Little Cleos, Krocodiles, Rapalas, and Rebels are popular lures; silver, blue and silver, orange and silver, green and silver, and gold are the standard lure finishes on Lake Champlain and should be in everyone's tackle box. Another very popular lure is the copper and silver Sutton spoon, which comes in many shapes and sizes. Multicolored flutter spoons, such as the Daredevle Flutter Chucks and the Evil Eye by Red Eye, have been very popular and productive in recent years. If you come to Lake Champlain to cast for the lake trout in the spring and fall, make sure you have a lot of red and white Daredevles and blue and silver Little Cleos in the ¼- to ¾-ounce sizes. They are among the most popular and most productive casting lures used on the lake. Even though I fish for all different species of cold-water and cool-water fish, in my opinion there is nothing quite like catching them on or near the surface. By using light tackle for surface fishing, you get at least twice the fight out of the fish as you would on heavy tackle in deep water.

Most people who troll for trout and salmon use spoons and minnow-imitating lures exclusively, but if you want to increase your success ratio, streamer flies are the answer. Whether you flatline or downrig, there are some days when using trolling flies could mean the difference between getting skunked or limiting out. When trolling in the spring and fall for trout and salmon, I use fly rods or ultralight spinning tackle with 4-pound leader or line with a number 3 or number 5 split shot about 18 inches up from the fly. Single or tandem flies in most smelt patterns will do. The most popular are the Grey Ghost, Green Ghost, Governor Akins, Joe's Smelt, Champlain Jane, and Nine Three, which are smelt patterns. The Mickey Finn and Edson Tiger, Golden Ghost, and Champlain Special are yellow patterns that, I believe, effectively represent the small perch that salmon and trout also feed on.

Night crawlers and smelt are the top natural live baits to use in Lake Champlain. Night crawlers and ground worms are cast out from the bank or boat and allowed to bounce along the bottom just as would be done in any trout stream. When bottom fishing with smelt, use a whole uncleaned smelt, which will float. Thread an English Gorge hook through the smelt and weight it with a slip sinker and split shot so that the smelt will float about a foot or two from the bottom. When drift-fishing in a boat, use a whole gutted smelt, which will sink. Hook it through the mouth and put a sinker about a foot above it.

Use a whole gutted smelt for tip-up fishing, but hook the bait by the dorsal fin so it will hang straight.

LAUNCHING AREAS

There are four major launching sites in the trout and salmon areas of the lake.

1. Point Au Roche Ramp, located a few miles north of Plattsburgh (Exits 35 and 36 off the Northway, Route 87)

2. Peru Dock, located a few miles south of Plattsburgh (Exits 35 and 36 off the Northway)

3. Willsboro Bay Launch Area (Exit 33 off the Northway)

4. Westport Launch Area (Exit 30 off the Northway)

All these are excellent launching areas with good ramps for almost any size boat and plenty of room for parking.

SHORE-FISHING AREAS

Except for the state park areas on Point Au Roche and Ausable Point, most shore-fishing areas are owned by the local towns or are privately owned. Moving from north to south these areas are:

1. Point Au Roche Park, located a few miles north of Plattsburgh (Northway Exit 40)

2. The mouth of the Saranac River, located in downtown Plattsburgh (Northway Exits 36 and 37)

3. Port Kent, cliff area just south of ferry landing (Northway Exit 34)

4. Willsboro Point, privately owned point with public access (Northway Exit 33)

5. Willsboro/Boquet River below Willsboro Dam (Northway Exit 33)

6. Essex Town Park, just south of Ferry Landing (Northway Exit 32)

7. Lachutte River Dam in Ticonderoga (Northway Exits 28 and 29)

The Port Kent and Essex areas are mainly used by smelt fishermen. No bait fishing is allowed on Willsboro Point. As mentioned above, most of these areas are not state owned, so these access areas can be taken away if we don't keep them neat and clean. They are strictly for fishing, so no camping or picnicking is allowed.

If you are fishing the Willsboro-Westport area, most accommodations and meals will be found right along Route 22. Route 9 has a number of restaurants and motels from Keeseville to Plattsburgh. This is the north country's big city, and it has many motels and restaurants. For a list of accommodations and eating establishments, contact these local chambers of commerce: Plattsburgh–North Country Chamber of Commerce, Plattsburgh, NY 12901 (518-563-1000); Ticonderoga Chamber of Commerce, Ticonderoga, NY 12883 (518-585-6619).

FISHING SEASONS AND REGULATIONS

Lake Champlain's trout and salmon season is year-round, generally including the tributaries up to the first barrier. The size limit for lake trout and salmon is 15 inches; for browns and rainbows it's 12 inches. To fish the New York side you'll need a New York license. Once you pass the boundary into Vermont, which is found in the middle of the lake, you will need a Vermont license. New York has approved a reciprocal license, but Vermont, so far, has balked at the idea. In any case, be sure to read the rules and regulations booklet that is issued with your New York State license. There is a specific section in the booklet on Lake Champlain.

Lake Champlain is probably the largest underfished lake in the country, and it offers variety that may not be matched anywhere. I believe the unique thing about Champlain's trout and salmon fishing is that you can fish for them a good 6 months of the year right on top—and isn't that the most enjoyable way of getting them?

ABOUT THE AUTHOR

Peter Casamento is a full-time licensed Adirondack guide and owner of the Adirondack-Champlain Guide Service in Willsboro. Specializing in the Adirondacks and Lake Champlain, he and the numerous other guides who work with him host more than 2,000 sportsmen each year. Peter resides in Willsboro on Long Pond with his wife Jane, daughter Crystal, and son Casey.

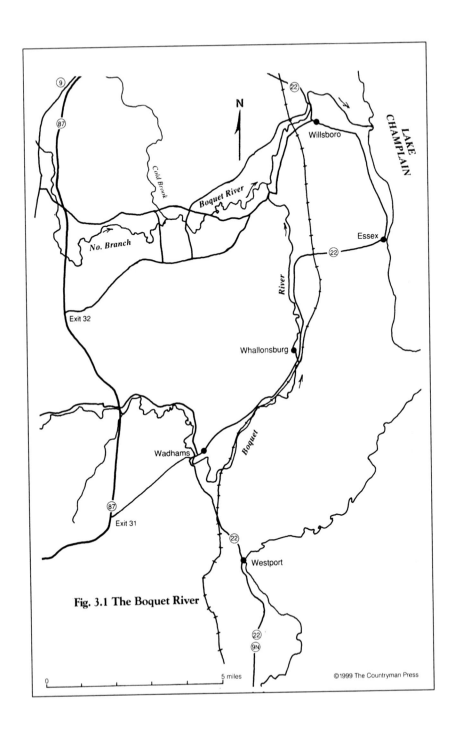

Fig. 3.1 The Boquet River

LAKE CHAMPLAIN

Willsboro

Essex

22

Boquet River

River

Cold Brook

No. Branch

Exit 32

Whallonsburg

Wadhams

Boquet

87
Exit 31

22

Westport

22
9N

9

87

N

0   5 miles

©1999 The Countryman Press

CHAPTER THREE

Salmon Fever!

KEN COLEMAN, WITH JIM HOTALING

O f all the great gamefish of North America, few have
inspired more admiration, storytelling, or sheer awe than
the Atlantic salmon, *Salmo salar*. An anadromous fish that lives
at sea and spawns annually in freshwater rivers of the northeast,
the Atlantic originally moved inland on its spawning runs up
rivers as far south as the Connecticut River. Over the past 200
years, though, many of the rivers between Maine and Connecticut became unsuitable for salmon because of pollution and
dams; for a long time the great battler was pushed northward to
New Brunswick, Labrador, and Quebec. During the past few
decades, however, titanic restoration efforts have reestablished
small but viable runs in some New England rivers, and the picture has been brightening slowly year by year.

Sometime during the last series of ice ages, *Salmo salar* was
cut off from the sea by geological changes, and an inland sub-
species developed: *Salmo salar sebago*. Happily, many of the same
qualities that evoke such passion in Atlantic salmon fishermen
are also exhibited by the landlocked salmon—streamlined good
looks, good fighting ability, a penchant for acrobatics, and a distinguished taste. The largest inland population of landlocks
developed in the Great Lakes, where the fish was later elimi-
nated or nearly so by human destruction of that watershed in
the 1800s and early 1900s. Similarly, the landlocks that occurred
naturally in other large bodies of water in the northeast—for

example, Lake Champlain—were extirpated by human activity by the mid- to late 1800s. Landlocks have been reintroduced to several waters in the Adirondacks, and in some of these, limited natural reproduction supported by stocking now occurs. Both Lake Champlain and Lake George offer landlocks, as do several other waters named later in this chapter. The major concentration of landlocked salmon in northern New York is in Lake Champlain and its major New York tributaries.

THE BOQUET RIVER

First and most important is the Boquet River. The Boquet flows from its source in the Adirondack Mountains better than 40 miles before it empties into Lake Champlain near Willsboro. Salmon can, with the help of the Willsboro Fish Ladder, ascend as far as the falls in Wadhams, about 12 miles from the lake. Willsboro is in Essex County, about 30 miles south of Plattsburgh and is considered by many to be the center of Lake Champlain's cold-water fishery.

There are two major runs of salmon in the Boquet River: in the spring and in the fall. There are also some minor runs periodically during the summer months. The spring run of salmon starts sometime in early to mid-April and will last into mid-June, with peak activity occurring in May. The spring run of salmon and trout is caused by the influx of warm water into Lake Champlain. These fish are entering the river to feed. Spring salmon can easily be caught on worms, lures, and flies. They usually run in the 2- to 3-pound range, although some spring salmon are caught in the 5- to 7-pound range. In addition to the salmon run, there is also a good run of brown trout.

The fall run of salmon starts around the second week of September and goes into the end of November. Peak activity is usually the last week of September through October.

Fall-run salmon enter the river for one reason: to spawn. When these fish first come upstream, they can be taken fairly easily. But after they have been in the river for a while, they become fussy and challenging. Persistence and patience will pay off. Fishing with nymphs and small wet flies using light leaders will work best.

A mixed catch of landlocks and steelhead from the Boquet.

The fall run of salmon won't have the numbers of fish like the spring run does, but the average size will be much larger. Fall salmon average 4–7 pounds, and there are many in the 8- to 12-pound range.

There are also some minor salmon runs in midsummer. These runs usually occur after a heavy rain and will last for about 3 or 4 days.

Of the Champlain tributaries, the Boquet offers the most mileage for fishing and has the most land open to public fishing. Upstream, the falls in Wadhams is a good spot to fish either flies or bait. There is parking along the road or in a lot just south of the bridge on Route 22. Start at the falls and work your way downstream. There are anglers' parking lots at most of the river crossings, and major pools with enticing water are numerous. Look for holding lies as you work along the stream (polarized glasses will help).

The North Branch (Fig. 3.1) splits off and offers several additional miles to the angler who enjoys wading and hunting for fish. These upper reaches of the Boquet do not get nearly the pressure the lower part of the river gets, but in turn, contain fewer fish than the lower part. The action picks up fast once you reach Willsboro. There is no fishing from the Route 22 bridge to the bottom of Willsboro Falls. This zone protects the fish as they go through the ladder, but the big pool at the foot of Willsboro Falls offers a great place to both fish and ogle at jumping fish as they move upstream. There is a parking lot on the south side of the river. The fish ladder was not built until the lampreys had taken their toll and the average size started dropping. Now, with lamprey control, the ladder may finally make the impact originally expected.

To fish the lower Boquet, head south on Route 22, cross the bridge, and turn left; then go by the school and the fish ladder to the lot. From here you can fish the main pool as well as several hundred feet of river below, and in the spring, this is as far as most fish come. Flies and bait are both used here, but day in and day out, more fish are taken on worms than anything else. If you do use a fly rod, this is a great place to fight a big fish.

There are several pools just downriver that offer good fly-fishing. Work the pools and riffs slowly with a Black Ghost, Grey

Ghost, Muddler Minnow, or your favorite salmon fly. An 8-foot or 8-foot-6-inch fly rod with 7- or 8-weight line is about right. As you move downriver, the water gets deeper and wider and a boat is needed.

To launch your boat, drive by the parking area to the end of the road, where there is another parking area and a place to launch a small boat or canoe. From here you can fish to the river mouth and into the lake. If you have a larger boat, you can put in at the state launch in Willsboro Bay on Lake Champlain and travel down the lake to the river mouth. You could also launch at the Essex Marina and go uplake to the river mouth.

A word of caution for those not familiar with Lake Champlain. On the "Big Lake"—and it is big, more than 100 miles long and 11 miles wide near Willsboro—either a south or north wind can blow up 4- or 5-foot waves in a hurry. Don't take it lightly. Boats of 16 feet or less should only be used near shore, and all boaters should keep an eye on the weather. If you can't make it back to the launch, pull into a sheltered bay and wait it out.

Small boats work fine in the river, but should be launched in the river. On a calm day, you can fish the Boquet and out into the lake as far as the marked buoy, and when the wind picks up, move back into the river. These delta areas at the river mouth are shallow and can be fished better by small boats. Bigger boats must be careful not to get hung up on the sandbars.

Watch for fish working on the surface, either cruising or jumping. Use light line and long rods and cast or troll up and down the river. Small spoons and flies or worms take the most fish here. Early morning or late evening is best, but fish can be taken all day long, and each rain or high water will bring more fish upstream.

One thing about fishing the mouth of the Boquet is that you never know what will hit next. I have taken several nice lake trout while trolling for salmon. As the salmon run comes to an end, smallmouth and walleye will move into the river, and even a few northerns will be taken at the river's mouth. Once other fish start moving into the river, the days of the salmon run are numbered.

THE AUSABLE AND SARANAC RIVERS

There are two other major salmon streams along the New York side of Lake Champlain. Like the Boquet, they too have their beginnings in the Adirondacks and flow into Lake Champlain.

The Ausable reaches the lake at Ausable Point in Clinton County. Salmon can only run a few miles upstream before coming to the impassable falls at Ausable Chasm, a popular tourist attraction on the edge of the village of Keeseville. The falls here are too high and will forever keep the upper reaches of the Ausable unavailable to salmon. Beyond the abilities of a fish ladder, the falls keep the Ausable limited as a salmon spawning stream.

On the Ausable, most of the land is now private, so wading space is hard to come by. Lots of nice fish, both salmon and trout, are taken off the Route 9 bridge. Spring and fall will find anglers fishing from the bridge. In fact, it is one of the first places I check to see if the fish are running. Worms are the most often used bait here. Flies will work in the big holes near the bridge, and some fishermen will bring their small boats all the way up here to fish just above or just below the bridge. At times they find fast action.

There is a small launch on Ausable Point Campsite Road, and small boats can be launched here or at the end of the point. Larger boats can be launched at the Peru Dock, a large state boat launch site just above the river on Route 9, across from Valcour Island. Lots of fishing takes place around the mouth of both the Ausable and the Little Ausable, which enters Champlain just to the north.

The third great tributary to Lake Champlain, the Saranac, winds its way from the Adirondacks through a series of small dams on its way to the lake. It offers a unique downtown fishery in Plattsburgh, and many nice trout and salmon are taken each year just across from City Hall. A fish ladder is scheduled to be built at Imperial Dam. It will allow salmon to travel for miles upriver to Kent Falls to spawn. The city has a walkway that gives good access all along the river within the city. The walkway means better access and more parking. There are plans for a boat launch site in the city of Plattsburgh at Wilcox Dock, once the chemical cleanup there takes place. This is badly needed;

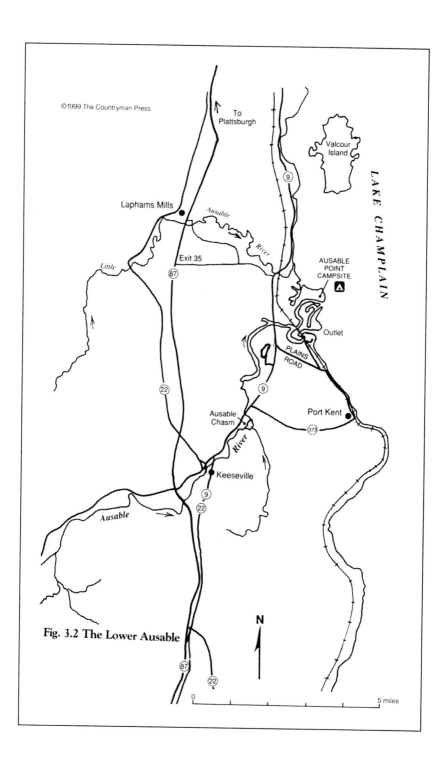

© 1999 The Countryman Press

To Plattsburgh

Valcour Island

LAKE CHAMPLAIN

Laphams Mills

Ausable

River

Little

Exit 35

⑧⑦

AUSABLE POINT CAMPSITE ⊿

Outlet

PLAINS ROAD

㉒

⑨

Ausable Chasm

Port Kent

㊼

River

Keeseville

⑨

㉒

Ausable

Fig. 3.2 The Lower Ausable

N

⑧⑦

㉒

0   5 miles

currently, the nearest launch for large boats is several miles away at either Point Au Roche to the north or the Peru Dock site to the south. Until a new boat launch site opens, the best spots to fish start at the old dam, which is always a good place to try and a favorite of many fly fishermen.

There are lots of other holes, with the next big favorite being along Pine Street, across from the grocery store and just up from the police station. There is a very large pool here, and lots of salmon are taken each year. As you move down, there is another good pool just upstream from Broad Street, behind the Tijuana Jail Restaurant. Next you come to the foot bridge just below the monument. When the fish are in, there will be plenty of fishermen working the pool from this bridge, and it makes a good place to check the action and see how the run is going. Just below the bridge is the only boat launch in the city. It will accommodate small to medium boats and offers parking for a limited number of cars. The launch is located on the south side of the river and offers the best access for fishing from here to the river mouth. There is no room to launch big boats—the ramp only accommodates car-toppers or boats 16 feet or smaller. It's a quick, safe way to fish the lower river, and believe me, when things are right, it pays off. If the fish are running, there will be several boats both anchored and trolling. Other anglers will be wading, fishing from shore, and hanging off the foot bridge. Nothing gets north country anglers more excited than the sight of a leaping salmon, and here is one place where you can see such action in the middle of town.

The lower reaches of all three rivers discussed can be fished by boat. As you work upstream, however, you encounter white water, and wading or bank fishing is indicated. There are good runs in both spring and fall, and the rivers can be easily fished without a guide. But for those who prefer to use a guide, they are available and can be of great help, particularly on your first trip. Inquire at any area bait and tackle shop.

Whatever your favorite fishing method, you can enjoy these great rivers. Trolling with a fly or spoon is popular off the river mouth or in the lower river. As you move upstream, many anglers switch to bait such as worms. Fly-fishing is very popular in the faster water near the upper reaches of each river.

Note: The Department of Environmental Conservation (DEC) has placed very restrictive regulations on these rivers (see the current New York State Fishing Regulations Guide). At this time it is not legal to use supplemental weights such as split shot, swivels, or wire leaders. Only unweighted baits or flies maybe used from the lake to the first impassable barrier. The one exception is the Saranac, where floating lures with one free-swinging hook may be used, and the no-weight regulations begin at the Catherine Street bridge, rather than at the river mouth.

LAKE CHAMPLAIN

For a few weeks each spring and fall, the rivers offer the best action, but don't overlook the salmon fishing in Lake Champlain. Chapter 2 discusses this, and I'll add only a few personal observations here.

Out on the open lake the fish have lots of room to run, jump, and generally keep your adrenaline flowing. Once in a while, you get one of those special days when the lake is calm and the salmon are right on top feeding on smelt, and this is your chance to fly-cast over big water. Use a good smelt pattern and make every cast count. With some luck, you can enjoy the ultimate—a fly-rod salmon with lots of room to run and jump. The speed of landlocked salmon is amazing, and don't be surprised if you lose more than you land; it's all part of the fun.

I think that one of the most important things to remember whenever you are fishing landlocked salmon is to keep your line light, 4- or 6-pound test, and keep your flies or spoons small. A number 12 Grey Ghost with one small weight on a 4-pound line can be a real killer. I believe oversized flies or lures with heavy line spook more salmon than anything else. Also important on the big lake is the use of planer boards to keep the line and lure off to the side. As your boat passes over salmon in shallow water or near the surface, they move to the side. The planer boards take the line to the side and give you a real shot at these fish. This method also lets you run a fly or lure through water too shallow to run your boat in.

OTHER SALMON WATERS

Lake Champlain is not the only Adirondack water with land-locks. Lake George, for example, is known to produce some really big fish. So is Schroon Lake and the Schroon River. Then, there is Upper Saranac Lake in Franklin County, Upper Chateaugay Lake in Clinton County, and Indian Lake in Hamilton County. All offer good landlocked salmon fishing.

For more information on Adirondack salmon fishing, contact the DEC in Ray Brook for the latest list of waters stocked with, and open to, landlocked salmon fishing. New water is stocked from time to time, and the DEC lists will keep you up to date. Some of the smaller salmon lakes, by the way, offer great fishing just after ice-out and provide an accommodating setting for the angler with a small boat.

ABOUT THE AUTHORS

Ken Coleman is a Michigan native who has called New York State home for the past 26 years. Currently a Plattsburgh resident, he is a retired real estate appraiser. In addition to writing about hunting and fishing, he has worked to promote the great outdoors through boat shows and through his work with guides and other outdoor professionals in the Adirondack region.

Jim Hotaling is a licensed guide and boat captain who owns the Champlain Angler in Willsboro and Trolling Tina Fishing Charters.

CHAPTER FOUR

The Mighty Saranac

JOHN SPISSINGER

Forget about what you think you're going to catch when you cast into the waters of New York's mighty Saranac River. Ply a small streamer for browns and rainbows in the deep turbulent pockets of the South Branch, and your fly might be ravaged by a hungry, deep-bodied smallmouth or by an angry northern pike. Troll slowly, or perhaps cast a jig for walleye in Union Falls Pond, and you might have to brace yourself for the dogged, powerful runs of a heavy, lake-reared brown trout. Lob a night crawler into the smooth currents at the mouth of the river in the city of Plattsburgh, and you just might be treated to the dazzling acrobatics of a fresh-run steelhead or landlocked salmon. Clearly, the rule of thumb to follow when fishing the mighty Saranac is "expect the unexpected."

The Saranac may be unique among Adirondack rivers in terms of the varied opportunities it presents to angling enthusiasts. Not only does it hold an interesting blend of cool- and cold-water gamefish, it also affords very different types of water that can be fished in different ways according to the individual preferences and skills of the angler. There is plenty of good water to suit the desires of spin, fly, and bait fishermen alike. Public access is excellent throughout the 65-mile stretch of river from Saranac Lake to Plattsburgh. Much of the river is navigable and can be fished from a canoe or small boat. Additionally, there is ample access for wading or bank fishing. Although

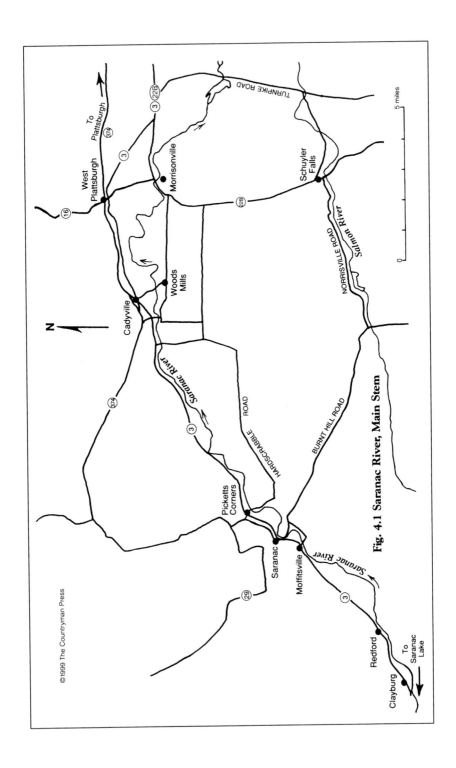

Fig. 4.1 Saranac River, Main Stem

©1999 The Countryman Press

there are a few seasonal hot spots where anglers tend to congregate, there's enough quality water spread throughout the river to ensure the peace and solitude that many anglers cherish. Combine these features, and you have a river that has something to offer every angler.

OVERVIEW

Located in the northeastern sector of New York's Adirondack Mountains, the Saranac flows easterly through parts of Franklin, Essex, and Clinton counties. Less heralded than its neighbor, the Ausable, the geography of the Saranac has much in common with that other great trout river. The headwaters of the Saranac and Ausable lie but a few miles apart in the High Peaks region of the Adirondack Park. The main stems of both rivers are formed by the confluence of their two branches: the East and West Branches of the Ausable, and the North and South Branches of the Saranac. With Lake Champlain their eventual destination, the rivers traverse roughly parallel courses before entering the lake less than 10 miles apart.

Unlike the Ausable, hydroelectric development has had a decisive impact on the Saranac's fishing. More than any other factor, the several hydroelectric impoundments along the Saranac account for the variety, abundance, and local intermingling of cold-, cool-, and warm-water species of fish. Anglers and environmentalists throughout the country have been rightfully concerned about the detrimental effects of such projects. Frequently, habitat is severely altered or destroyed, and some species of fish are totally eradicated. Occasionally, though, hydro projects have actually had a positive impact on fishery resources by creating or improving habitat. Arguably, the Saranac is one of those watersheds that has benefited from its hydro impoundments. Supporting this contention are the fine walleye and smallmouth populations that have developed behind some of its dams and the establishment of very good brown trout fisheries in the tailwaters below the dams, particularly below the Kent Falls dam. Presently, there are nine hydro projects on the Saranac. From a recreational standpoint, the best fishing opportunities are found at Franklin and Union Falls Ponds on the

Nine-year-old Karalyn Aprill with a walleye.

South Branch and in the waters above the Kent Falls, Mill C, and Cadyville dams on the main stem. Some of the most varied fishing on the Saranac system takes place in the waters above these dams.

Franklin Falls Pond and Union Falls Pond are both rather sizable bodies of water. Franklin Falls Pond spreads over 435 acres and has a maximum depth of 30 feet. Larger still, Union

Falls Pond encompasses 1,575 acres but is slightly shallower at 20 feet. Both ponds are classified as warm-water fisheries by the Department of Environmental Conservation (DEC). (More and more people are using the more accurate phrase *cool-water species*, and that is the one we use in this book.) An excellent walleye fishery exists in Union Falls Pond, which is stocked heavily with this species. The walleyes are not large, but they are plentiful. Occasional fish are taken in the 6–8-pound range. Franklin Falls Pond also supports a walleye population, but it has yet to reach its full potential. However, DEC remains quite optimistic about the prospects for walleye in Franklin Falls, in part because its habitat for this species is actually better than Union Falls.

In addition to walleye, northern pike are prevalent in both ponds. Again, while the fish are not huge, they are abundant and provide excellent sport. Fish in the 10- to 12-pound range have been taken, and there are probably some larger specimens lurking in the depths. Smallmouth are also present in good numbers, and there are enough 3- to 5-pounders around to keep things interesting. You would not want to fish either Franklin or Union Falls Ponds if brown trout were your primary quarry. Each year, however, both ponds surrender some very large browns that take up residence in the still waters. Besides the gamefish, yellow perch, bullhead, and other panfish provide both action and excellent tablefare. A few of the perch grow to a foot or more, and during the winter they, along with the walleye and northerns, attract a popular following of ice fishermen.

Getting to Franklin or Union Falls Ponds is relatively easy. The River Road in Bloomingdale, the Cold Brook Road in Vermontville, and the Alder Brook Road at the junction of County Route 26 all lead into the area from the south side of Route 3. Yet another route to take, especially if you've been fishing the Ausable, is to drive north on the Silver Lake Road in Ausable Forks to the Union Falls Road near Silver Lake.

While private camps dot the shorelines of both ponds, there are plenty of places to fish once there. At Franklin Falls, there are several roadside pull-offs and paths that lead down to the shoreline. Although there are no trailer launch sites, it is quite easy to get into the pond with a canoe or small car-top boat, especially near the dam. Similar access is available on Union Falls Pond. In addition, there is a private launch site and boat livery near the end of the impoundment. If you fish Franklin Falls, don't neglect the deep, slow-water stretch below the dam. Sometimes the walleye, northern, and smallmouth fishing here is as good as on the main lake. However, caution should be used when fishing along the steep ledges and rocks above the gorge. Similarly, it is also prudent to be cautious when boating in Union and Franklin Falls as there are boulders and stumps throughout these impoundments. It's a good idea to speak with fellow anglers or to seek the advice of the proprietor of the launch on Union Falls to learn where the channels and hazards lie, as well as where the seasonal hot spots are.

FISHING ON THE LOWER SARANAC

The fishing opportunities above the three dams on the lower Saranac, near Cadyville, are similar to those described at Franklin and Union Falls Ponds. Here, though, smallmouth attract the most attention while northerns and walleye play a somewhat lesser role. The reservoirs above the Kent Falls and Mill C dams are quite narrow, at most a few hundred yards wide, and short, about ½ mile long. Behind the Cadyville dam the river is backed up for several miles, although it remains narrow.

Because the Cadyville, Mill C, and Kent Falls dams are not more than 2 miles apart, it's easy to sample the fishing at each spot on a single day. Route 3 passes alongside the Cadyville reservoir, and intersections with the Harvey Bridge and Goddeau Roads provide access to the Mill C and Kent Falls reservoirs. The New York State Electric and Gas Company (NYSEG) maintains parking areas on both waters. It is possible to put in a canoe or small car-top boat at these sites, though most of the fishing is done from the shore. The village of Cadyville maintains a small recreational area, including a trailer launch facility, right off Route 3. While parking is limited by the size of this facility, it remains a popular access site. Between Cadyville and Saranac, about 7 miles upstream, there are several intersecting roads that provide additional access. Some local anglers like to float this stretch, launching their canoes at the

Hardscrabble Road bridge in Saranac and drifting downstream to the Cadyville beach where a second car is left.

TROUT FISHING

The Saranac's reputation as a blue-ribbon trout river is borne out in the productive pools, riffles, and pocket water above and below the several impoundments. Trout fishing enthusiasts can easily explore and sample these stretches by taking a leisurely drive along Route 3, starting either in Plattsburgh or in Saranac Lake. About one-third of the South Branch, half of the North Branch, and virtually all of the main stem border this highway. There are many parking areas along the river that allow you to make close-up inspections of promising stretches of water. Moreover, additional information can be gleaned from local sources, like the bait and tackle shops, small grocery stores, inns, and campgrounds that are evident along Route 3. Assuming that you're leaving from Saranac Lake, the following paragraphs should give a picture of what to look for as you head downstream.

From the Lake Flower dam to the hamlet of Bloomingdale, the South Branch wanders through meadows and swampland. Road access is relatively limited along this slow, deep run, and floating it by canoe is probably the best approach. Although a few trout are stocked in the village of Saranac Lake on a put-and-take basis, smallmouth and northerns are more numerous. Just before Bloomingdale, the river veers away from Route 3 and quickens its tempo as it flows through pine and hardwood forests. Good access is found along the River Road in Bloomingdale, which follows the river downstream to Franklin Falls Pond. Generally, the faster slicks and pocket water hold brown and rainbow trout while a mixed bag is to be found in the slower pools and runs. After passing through Franklin and Union Falls Ponds, the South Branch resumes its course and is largely inaccessible until it crosses the Silver Lake Road bridge. The river is heavily posted and patrolled on both sides of the bridge, but there are three public fishing/parking areas just north of the bridge down to the junction with Route 3 in Clayburg. Anglers must descend steep banks to get to the river

A view of the often tumbling Saranac River, below the rapids at Redford. This young angler will be tested by the heavy water.

from these sites, but the excellent brown and rainbow fishing is worth the effort. This is a turbulent, boulder-strewn section with many deep pockets. Calmer waters are not to be found until the river merges with the North Branch in Clayburg.

For the beauty, solitude, and enchantment that so many anglers feel to be the essence of trout fishing, few Adirondack rivers can match the charms of the Saranac's North Branch. It is a cold, quiet little river from its headwaters to its junction with the brawling South Branch in Clayburg. Dense, overhanging alders, waist-deep oxbow bends, and undercut banks provide ideal cover for the brook, brown, and rainbow trout that thrive in its waters. The North Branch is easy to get to from several well-maintained public parking areas on Route 3, from Clayburg 5 miles upstream to Alder Brook. During May and June, this stretch sees some moderate to heavy angling pressure. Yet few anglers bother to fish the headwaters of the North Branch, which can be reached via the Goldsmith Road (which joins Route 3 a few miles west of Alder Brook). The river is much smaller here, in places no more than a few feet wide, and thickly forested. Native brookies are small but plentiful, and occasional wild browns are an added bonus. Although there are a number of private camps and posted property along the Goldsmith Road, DEC has secured public fishing rights in various spots. The fish are highly selective on the North Branch, and often you have to work hard to catch them. Still, there are few places anywhere in the region that look as intriguing as the North Branch of the Saranac.

Reasonably good trout water continues on the main stem of the river from Clayburg to Saranac, 6 miles downstream. Because the river is so broad and shallow here, it doesn't appear to be a productive reach of water. However, the choppy riffles disguise deeper subsurface trenches and pockets. Trout hold in these protected areas and migrate to feed along the shallower edges. Although it takes practice to learn how to read this water, some surprisingly good fishing can be had. Several riverside parking areas are present along this stretch. Generally, the Hardscrabble Road bridge in Saranac marks the dividing line between cold- and cool-water species. Shortly below the bridge the effects of the Cadyville dam are evident, and smallmouth, northerns, walleye, and panfish displace the trout.

The final stretch of trout water worth mentioning on the Saranac lies between the Kent Falls dam and the village of Morrisonville. Here the river is broad and fast flowing, with subsurface runs and pockets interspersed among a few deep pools. Caution should be exercised when fishing this stretch, because the water level fluctuates significantly during periods of power generation. The swift currents and loose cobble bottom combine to make wading tricky under any circumstances. The Kent Falls Road borders the river from Route 22B in Morrisonville upstream to the dam. NYSEG maintains a fisherman's parking area below the powerhouse, and some roadside pull-offs give access farther downstream.

BEST SEASONS TO FISH

Because it is such a large and varied river, the best time of year to fish the Saranac pretty much depends on what you hope to catch and where you plan to go. June and September are probably the best months for both cool- and cold-water species. Although trout season remains open on a year-round basis, the action is usually better on the lower sections of the main stem in late April and early May, and then improves upstream as the waters warm. During the hottest days of summer the North Branch, with its shaded waters and many spring seepages, is a good bet. Walleyed and northern pike fishing above the dams is best right after the season opens in mid-May through June, and then again in the fall. Not to be forgotten is the occasionally excellent ice fishing on Union Falls Pond in February. Smallmouth fishing remains consistently good from opening day in June through October.

FISHING TIPS

If the fish are in a cooperative mood, the flies, lures, and baits that work well for the different species elsewhere are also usually productive on the Saranac. Worms provide the most action as there's not a fish in the river that won't gobble one up from time to time. Live or salted minnows will reduce the number of strikes by nuisance fish like river chubs and improve chances for a good-sized northern, walleye, smallmouth, or brown. Small jigs, spinnerbaits, plugs, and crankbaits also work well for these species. Fly fishermen will encounter many of the major eastern mayfly hatches starting with the Hendricksons in early to mid-May. The green drake hatch, which begins in early June on the lower river and moves upstream in successive weeks, can be phenomenal. Actually, some of the best smallmouth fishing occurs when this fly is on the water above the dams. Trout will often ignore these juicy morsels and instead feed heavily on smaller caddis flies. But smallmouth find the drakes irresistible and will smash them with a vengeance. Large stonefly nymphs are productive in the South Branch's pocket water, while terrestrial imitations and midges pay off on the North Branch in summer. As searching patterns, the traditional Adams, Muddlers, Hare's Ear nymphs, Ausable Wulffs, and some elk-hair caddis flies tied in various colors and sizes will be useful in most situations. With fly patterns as with lures and baits, it's always prudent to compare notes with fellow anglers to learn what seems to be the hot pick at any given time.

SALMON AND STEELHEAD

Although the city of Plattsburgh marks the end of the Saranac's journey toward Lake Champlain, it is also the site of the newest —and to many the most exciting—dimension of the river's diverse menu. In the 1960s New York's DEC began experimental stockings of landlocked salmon in Lake Champlain's major tributaries. Historical records indicate that salmon were once native to the lake, but pollution, overharvesting, and destruction of spawning habitat led to their demise by the mid-19th century. Results of the initial restorative stockings were encouraging as the salmon thrived on the abundant forage base in the lake and then returned to spawn in the lower reaches of the tributaries. The stockings continued throughout the 1970s and 1980s and were augmented by the introduction of steelhead trout. Today, the Saranac supports moderately good runs of salmon and steelhead. With eel controls now in effect, the prospects for the future will be even brighter, especially with plans under way to construct a fish ladder at the Imperial Mill Dam in the city of Plattsburgh. The ladder should be in place by the year 2000, opening up 10 additional miles of river for the fish and increasing access for anglers.

Salmon and steelhead fishing on the lower Saranac is very different from that found on Lake Ontario's tributaries. Unlike the monstrous chinook and coho salmon of Lake Ontario, Lake Champlain's steelhead range from 16–20 inches, with some larger specimens weighing more than 4 pounds. Another key difference between Lake Ontario's Pacific salmon and Lake Champlain's landlocks is that landlocked salmon do not die after spawning but return to the lake to feed, grow larger, and

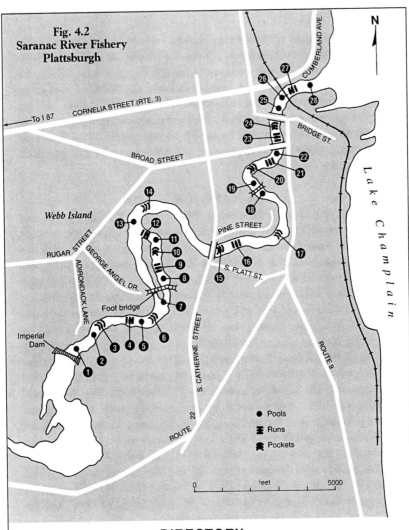

Fig. 4.2
Saranac River Fishery
Plattsburgh

Webb Island

Imperial Dam

Foot bridge

- Pools
- Runs
- Pockets

0   feet   5000

DIRECTORY

1. Imperial Mill Pool	8. Footbridge Pool	15. S. Catherine St. Pockets	22. Kennedy Bridge Pool
2. Cable Pool	9. Upper Webb Run	16. Lee's Run	23. Durkee St. Run
3. Adirondack Pockets	10. Webb Island Pockets	17. Pine St. Pockets	24. Durkee St. Pockets
4. Underwood Run	11. Big Bend Pool	18. Millie's Pool	25. Bridge St. Pool
5. Football Field Pool	12. Lower Webb Run	19. Police Station Pool	26. Band Shell Pool
6. Lower Field Pockets	13. Allen St. Pool	20. Jailhouse Pockets	27. Railroad Trestle Run
7. Angie's Pool	14. Dorm Pockets	21. Coal Hole Run	28. Delta Mouth Pool

then spawn again. For this reason, catching salmon by snagging or lifting is strictly prohibited on the Saranac. (Anglers should consult the *New York State Fishing Regulations Guide* to learn the special regulations in effect on the lower Saranac.) Although it will never offer salmon that match in either size or number the Pacific salmon that ascend Lake Ontario's Salmon River each fall, the Saranac offers a qualitatively different angling experience more akin to traditional Atlantic salmon fishing. And the land-locks are no less spectacular fighters than their seagoing cousins.

The Saranac's spring salmon run usually begins in early April and continues through mid-May, depending on the water temperature and level. The best fishing occurs from the river's mouth to perhaps ½ mile upstream. Although not particularly large at this time of year, averaging between 16 and 20 inches, the salmon are voracious feeders and will hit worms, spoons, plugs, streamers, nymphs, and even dry flies. More important than what to use is the task of getting your lure, bait, or fly down near the bottom in the swift, heavy waters. Fly-fishing anglers should come equipped with at least a 7-weight rod system and either a full-sinking or fast-sink-tip line. Spin and bait anglers would do well to use a long sturdy rod and reel with a dependable drag. Six- to 8-pound-test line will normally handle the most challenging fish.

Early September marks the beginning of the fall spawning migration, with the peak coming by mid-October. The salmon ascend the river as far as the Imperial Mill dam 3 miles upstream. The fish are both larger and more temperamental than in the spring because they are not actively feeding. Patience, in the form of repetitive casts into likely pools and runs, is the only sure way to maximize chances for success. When the salmon are inclined to hit, they will strike almost anything. Worms and plugs continue to work, although fly-fishing is perhaps more successful in fall. Some anglers have luck using traditional Atlantic salmon flies, with the Cosseboom and Rusty Rat being notable favorites. The majority of fly-fishing enthusiasts use streamers and bucktails. Yellow maribou streamers, Grey Ghosts, and Muddlers, in sizes 2–8, are popular patterns. Again, however, the exact pattern seems less important than the mood of the fish at any given moment.

Because the lower Saranac flows directly through the city of Plattsburgh, access is not a problem. Following Route 3 or Route 9 into the downtown section will lead to the mouth of the river. There are plans for a boat launch at Wilcox Dock just north of the mouth of the Saranac. The work will start after the DEC cleanup of the sludge bed there, perhaps as early as the year 2000. Ample parking is available, and there is access for handicapped anglers as well. A small trailer launch facility can be found near the city's municipal treatment plant. For the present, however, access to the Imperial Pool and to other productive stretches is gained either by parking in back of the college fieldhouse and walking down to the river, or by taking George Angell Drive to the footbridge in back of the Plattsburgh High School. Both areas are located off Rugar Street near the SUNY–Plattsburgh campus. Fall fishing can be quite congested at times, but this should change when the fish ladder at Imperial Dam is completed in 1999, opening up more water and thereby distributing the pressure.

For all the excitement that surrounds the Saranac's salmon run, anglers should still never be too sure about what they'll catch when they give it a try. Steelhead, smallmouth, walleye, northerns, brown trout, and even lakers swim in the same water as the migrant landlocks. And they hit just often enough to remind everyone of the truth of the proposition that when fishing the mighty Saranac, it's always best to "expect the unexpected!"

ABOUT THE AUTHOR

John Spissinger is a trout bum of the first order. John lives in Peru, New York, and has served as secretary and most recently as regional director of Trout Unlimited. An ardent fly tier, John has taught fly-tying classes for the past 18 years for Trout Unlimited members in the Plattsburgh area.

CHAPTER FIVE

The Legendary Ausable

FRANCIS BETTERS

A book on fishing in the Adirondacks must include a chapter on the fabled West Branch of the Ausable River, which emanates from the highest peaks in the Adirondacks and, after joining the river's other main branch, flows eventually into Lake Champlain. The 30-mile-long West Branch is considered by many top outdoor writers and a multitude of anglers who have visited it to be one of the best trout streams in the East. Man with all his wisdom and technical skill could not have drawn a better blueprint for the perfect trout stream than Mother Nature has provided in the West Branch of the Ausable.

THE WEST BRANCH

The Ausable River consists of two main branches, but it is the West Branch that has received the most attention, and rightfully so. It is this branch to which thousands of fly and spin fishermen from all over the United States and many foreign countries come to try their luck at hooking one of the lunker brown trout that inhabit the many deep pools found here.

To understand why the West Branch is so good, it is important to know what ingredients go into producing a premier trout stream. This in turn necessitates knowing what the trout's requirements are—that is, what it takes to ensure an abundant and healthy population of fish. To sum these requirements up

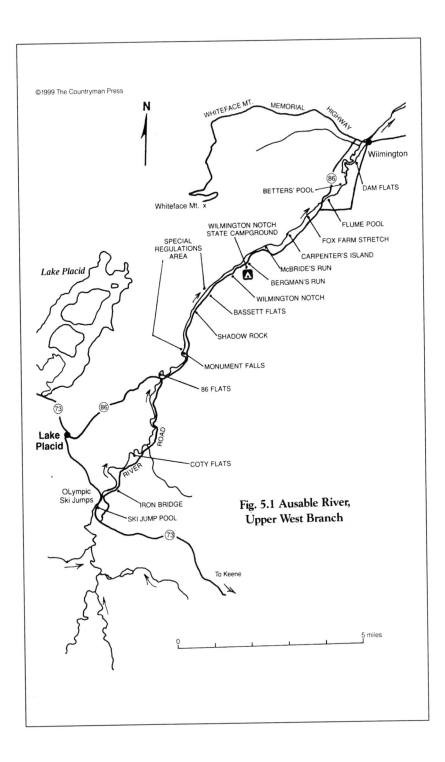

N

WHITEFACE MT. MEMORIAL HIGHWAY

Wilmington

Whiteface Mt. x

BETTERS' POOL

DAM FLATS

FLUME POOL

FOX FARM STRETCH

CARPENTER'S ISLAND

WILMINGTON NOTCH STATE CAMPGROUND

McBRIDE'S RUN

BERGMAN'S RUN

WILMINGTON NOTCH

SPECIAL REGULATIONS AREA

BASSETT FLATS

SHADOW ROCK

Lake Placid

MONUMENT FALLS

86 FLATS

Lake Placid

ROAD

RIVER

COTY FLATS

OLympic Ski Jumps

IRON BRIDGE

SKI JUMP POOL

Fig. 5.1 Ausable River, Upper West Branch

To Keene

0   5 miles

briefly: (1) unpolluted water, (2) a proper temperature range and a good supply of oxygen, (3) a plentiful food supply, and (4) cover.

How does the West Branch stack up in each of these four categories?

The water is still very clean in spite of increasing development in the area, and there are no great pollution problems menacing the river. The rich mineral water from the mountain feeder streams and the rich soil that is found along parts of the West Branch provide a good foundation for the food chain that eventually feeds the trout. The river provides good nourishment for both of the major sources of food the trout feed on, namely insects and bait fish.

Traversing a very cold part of the Adirondacks, the West Branch usually runs in a favorable temperature range for the trout. The shady conditions brought on by steep gorges and overhanging foliage help out in this regard, so that even in summer, the West Branch is often surprisingly chilly. As for the oxygen content, it is very good, thanks in part to the steep gradient. An abundant supply of oxygen is infused into the river as the water tumbles over the millions of rocks and boulders that make up the stream bottom in a large part of the West Branch.

The lower forms of life that the trout feed on are found in large numbers. The Ausable has an abundance of all three of the most important species of insects: mayflies, stoneflies, and caddis flies. These insects are a good source of protein, and their abundance promotes good trout growth.

Finally, in terms of cover, the West Branch is hard to beat. Not only are there many deep pools, but there are a multitude of hiding and holding spots created by rocks and boulders and, in places, undercut banks.

It might be added here that another virtue of the Ausable is its very remoteness. It is far from any of the major cities of the East, and this has so far prevented overuse. Also, it is one of the most heavily stocked rivers in New York State.

The West Branch begins its fetal stage in the mountains. The headwaters comprise several brooks that flow essentially north from the Mount Marcy High Peaks area. As these tumbling mountain brooks converge, they gather strength, and at

A happy angler.

the junction of March Brook and South Meadow Brook, the West Branch is officially born. This is at the western edge of the South Meadows area and just south of the village of Lake Placid. The West Branch then winds its way down past the Olympic ski jumps just outside Lake Placid, picking up Indian Pass Brook on the way.

For the next 4 or 5 miles, the river is fairly calm as it makes its way through more meadowland, picking up a number of other small feeder streams. This is the part I refer to as the "Sweetwater" section of the Ausable. The river continues to grow, reaching the Route 86 bridge about 3 miles north of Lake Placid. After this crossing, the river really begins to gain character, passing through its rebellious and energetic teenage stage, if you will. A few miles farther downstream, ancient glaciers have carved out a series of deep gorges in what is now called Wilmington Notch. As it tumbles through these gorges, the river takes on the mature personality by which it is chiefly known. The rocky West Branch is extremely scenic here, with one of the most dramatic spots being about a mile upstream of the Wilmington Notch State Campground. Here, the river roars over a falls that is more than 100 feet high. Through the millennia, the countless billions of gallons of water churning over this great falls (called High Falls) have gouged out a deep pool within which large trout can hide amid the boulders and ledges. The trout here are comparatively safe both from anglers and from the large chunks of ice that come crashing down each spring when the ice breaks up in the slower sections upriver.

For the next 2 miles, the river sort of catches its breath as it forms numerous pools and pockets before taking another spectacular plunge over another series of falls known today as "the Flume." Beneath this falls, there is another large, deep pool that has become famous over the years and where big trout are taken each spring after ice-out. There is rarely a day during the open trout season when there aren't fishermen lining the ledges along both sides of this pool. Surprisingly, in spite of the pressure most of them catch some fish. Over the years, I have taken many good trout in the 15- to 20-inch range and can recall a half-dozen or more lunkers that weighed from 4 to 7 pounds. My largest was a 7¼-pound brown taken on a Hornberg streamer.

About a mile below the Flume Falls, the river seems to rest after its arduous journey, and it flows now in a more peaceful fashion until it eventually meets the constraint of a dam located in the center of Wilmington. This is what most of the old-time residents of the village refer to as Lake Everest, but it is merely a dammed up section of stream about 2 miles long, 100 to 400-feet wide, and about 20 feet deep. This beat of the West Branch holds some lunkers, and each spring one or two very large trout are bested by lucky anglers fishing the local beach. Recently, for example, an 8 ½-pounder was taken by one of the local residents. This 2-mile section of slow water above the dam is an ideal spot for bait fishermen, but aside from the section between the bridge in town and the dam, and the small beach section, it must be fished from a small boat.

Beneath this dam at Wilmington, another large pool measuring some 400 feet across holds a great many trout, with some weighing more than 3 pounds. A fairly adept fly fisherman can wade out near the center of the stream below the pool and cast up toward the dam. It is an ideal place to fish large streamers and weighted nymphs. It's also a good spot to try big dry flies just before dark, and in the spring after ice-out, it is one of the favorite pools of bait fishermen.

The section from the Wilmington dam downstream about 2 miles is my favorite stretch for fly-fishing. Here there are pools too numerous to count and pockets formed by converging currents around boulders, and these create excellent fly-fishing water. Access here is difficult, however.

After the river crosses beneath Lewis Bridge below Wilmington, no fishing is allowed for about 1 ½ miles. Fortunately, this is not one of the better parts of the West Branch. The river here is fairly wide and shallow for the most part, with only a few good holding pools. But from where Black Brook empties into the river at the lower end of the posted water, the river again has an increased number of pools and pockets, and these persist for the next 6 or 7 miles. This beat of river from Black Brook to Ausable Forks is known as "the Bush Country." There are numerous old logging roads from which one can reach the river, but for the most part it has to be reached by foot. New subdivisions and posting have made access here more and more

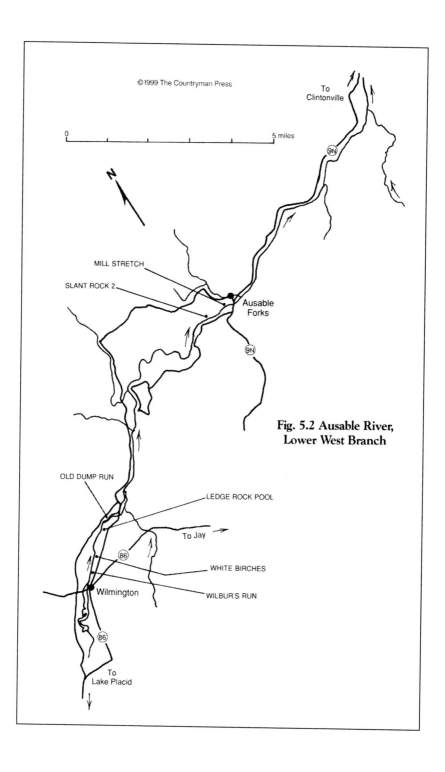

© 1999 The Countryman Press

0   5 miles

To Clintonville

N

9N

MILL STRETCH

SLANT ROCK 2

Ausable Forks

9N

Fig. 5.2 Ausable River, Lower West Branch

OLD DUMP RUN

LEDGE ROCK POOL

To Jay

86

WHITE BIRCHES

WILBUR'S RUN

Wilmington

86

To Lake Placid

Fishing the pocket water on one of the prime sections of the West Branch, several miles north of Lake Placid along Route 86.

difficult. As with the dammed-up section at Wilmington, the ½-mile impounded part of the West Branch above the dam at Ausable Forks contains many trophy-sized fish.

For about a mile below this dam at Ausable Forks, the West Branch offers up some excellent pocket water for the fly fisherman. It is, however, one of the roughest sections of the river to wade. Its bottom is littered with segments of old bridges, broken boulders, and pieces of cement blasted out when the old pulp mills were destroyed years ago.

Let's now get a little bit more specific about a few of the better sections of the West Branch.

The stretch from the Olympic ski jump outside the village of Lake Placid down to the Route 86 bridge is for the most part deep water with undercut banks, some faster currents, and a few pools. It may be that the largest trout in the stream are hiding beneath these undercut banks. The Department of Environmental Conservation (DEC) once shocked one of the larger pools in this section and turned up three trout weighing more than 6 pounds apiece. (This same scenario also occurs in the mile-long section from the Route 86 bridge down to Monument Falls, where the trophy section begins.) This section is best fished with nymphs, small streamers, or large wet flies during the early-season months. At this time, bait fishermen can excel on this part of the river. During the warmer summer months, small flies in sizes 18–22 work best. Terrestrials such as ants and grasshoppers can be a good choice during the summer period, too. There is also an excellent trico hatch here in August and September.

From the beginning of the trophy section (discussed below) at Monument Falls all the way down to the Flume, the river is broken water with plenty of pockets and pools. Much of this is wadable fly-fishing water, and it is very good. Another of my favorite stretches is the approximately 1-mile section below the Flume. Here there are a number of islands below which large pools have been formed. These pools produce good-sized trout each spring and fall. This particular section is about 200 feet off Route 86, just north of the Flume bridge.

SEASONS AND TIPS

Many wonder what the best fishing periods are for the various types of fishing possible on the West Branch. From April 1 when the general season opens until about the middle of May is when bait fishermen often do best. The best natural baits are minnows and worms. In the faster sections of the West Branch, spinners are often the most effective spinning lures. Included here would be Panther Martins, Mepps, Roostertails, C.P. Swings, or Swiss Swings, etcetera. In the medium to slower sections, Phoebes and Rapalas are often deadly, but they do not operate as well as spinners in the white water. Fly fishermen during this same early period will do best using small streamers and nymphs fished deep, because the trout are not as active in the cold water and will be close to the bottom. Good early-season patterns are the Grey Ghost, Muddler Minnow, Woolly Worm, and Hornberg.

The best fly-fishing months for the dry-fly fisherman are May, June, July, and September into the middle of October. The first major hatch to emerge is the Hendrickson, between the 5th and 10th of May. It is well to remember that the mayfly hatches on the Ausable come off about 2 weeks later than they do on Catskill streams because of the higher elevation and the colder water temperatures. There are heavy hatches of caddis flies during May and June and good hatches of stoneflies throughout the season. The longest hatch of the year is the *Isonychia bicolor,* which comes off beginning around the middle of August and lasts well into October.

Because much of the river is made up of fast water with many boulders and heavy currents, the most productive flies are usually the larger ones (sizes 10, 12, and 14); smaller flies are often the ticket in the slicks and the pools. The fly that seems to account for more fish than any other is my own Ausable Wulff in sizes 10 and 12. Some of the other especially productive patterns are the dark and light Haystacks, light and dark caddis flies, Light Cahill, Adams, March Brown, and Hendrickson. The most productive nymph patterns are the black, brown, and light stonefly nymphs, gray mayfly, all-purpose light, Light Cahill, Hendrickson, and blue dun. During July and August, small midges and terrestrials are in order. A good imitation for the *Isonychia* dun is the Dark Haystack with a reddish-brown body.

Another aspect of fishing on the West Branch worth mentioning is the ratio of stocked fish to those spawned in the stream. In the center section of the stream, between Wilmington and the Olympic ski jumps, the trout are mostly stocked fish. A very high percentage of these fish are brown and rainbow trout. From the Olympic ski jump upstream, there is a greater percentage of wild speckled trout (in smaller sizes). From the dam in Wilmington downstream, you will also find a greater percentage of naturally spawned trout, mostly browns and rainbows, but a fair number of speckled trout as well. This 6- or 7-mile section from the dam downstream is the most productive water on the river. Here is where you will find the best fly hatches from May through September.

A word of special advice is in order in regard to wading the

West Branch of the Ausable. The river has one of the slipperiest bottoms I have ever encountered, thanks to the algae that covers the rocks, in many areas of the stream. Combine this with the large and often jagged rocks and you can see why the West Branch is such a treacherous river to wade. It is wise to use both a wading staff and felt-soled waders or felt-soled wading shoes.

REGULATIONS

For the most part, the West Branch is governed by general statewide trout regulations—10 trout per day, no size limit, with the season running from April 1 to September 30. However, there are two special regulations sections. The first is from the Route 86 bridge northeast of Lake Placid downstream to the Wilmington Dam. Here you can take 10 trout 9 inches or larger by any legal method, and the season is year-round. Section two lies within section one. This is the beat from Monument Falls downstream 2¼ miles, usually called the trophy section. Within this zone you may keep only three trout 12 inches or larger, and you may use artificial lures only. Again, the season is year-round.

Since the trophy section was initiated some dozen years ago, it has become a very popular part of the river. Although the trout do not average much larger than those in the remainder of the stream, the DEC does stock this section from time to time with some of its large breeders. A couple of years ago, they put in about 800 large rainbows weighing up to 8 pounds. During the regular trout season, there is probably at least one large trout taken each week from the trophy section.

Another dimension has recently been added to the West Branch of the Ausable. Three years ago, the trophy section was extended and part of it was converted to a catch-and-release area, making a total of 5 miles of catch and release. This area is stocked a number of times each year with trout in the 15-inch range or larger. It has become a very popular section of river for both the novice angler and for those wishing to catch trout without so much of a challenge. Although this section is at times overfished, it produces some excellent opportunities to test your skills at hooking and landing some good-sized trout.

Perhaps the best spin-off from this 5-mile section is that it reduces pressure on the better sections of the river below the dam at Wilmington.

Be aware that this 5-mile section of catch and release is not limited to fly-fishing only. It's a good place to take novice spin fishermen as well. It's recommended that those fishing with spinning rods use a single-hook lure to make it easier to release the fish. Small spinner flies work exceptionally well. Remember that bait is prohibited in this section.

THE MAIN STEM

Just downstream of the bridge in the center of Ausable Forks, the West Branch converges with its sister stream, the East Branch, to form the main Ausable. Although the main branch contains some trout, it is not considered top-quality trout water. The river is quite wide and shallow for the most part, and it contains a large number of chubs and shiners. A few good pools can be found farther downstream, but as the river is quite shallow, it heats up during the hot summer months and doesn't produce well. Nonetheless, the Main Stem of the Ausable has its devotees, and there are trout to be caught.

THE EAST BRANCH

The East Branch of the Ausable has its origins in the Ausable Lakes area, southwest of the village of Keene Valley. It flows northward along Route 9N past the villages of Keene, Jay, and Upper Jay. It is a good trout stream by most standards, but pales alongside the West Branch, in terms of both numbers and size of the trout. The East Branch is relatively shallow, without much character, and during the hot months of July and August does not produce well. It is, though, a much tamer river than the West Branch and therefore much easier to wade. There are some good holding pools, and the stream is a good choice for the less adventurous and less aggressive fisherman.

The deeper holding pools and runs are few and far between, so you will have to explore a greater section of the stream to find them. One nice stretch is from Keene upstream

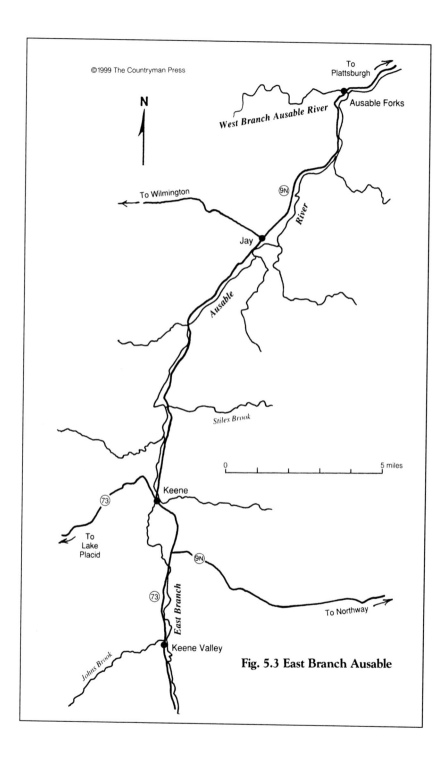

N

To Plattsburgh

West Branch Ausable River

Ausable Forks

To Wilmington

9N

River

Jay

Ausable

Stiles Brook

0   5 miles

Keene

73

To Lake Placid

9N

73

East Branch

To Northway

Johns Brook

Keene Valley

Fig. 5.3 East Branch Ausable

to Hull's Falls. Unlike the West Branch, the East Branch has few good feeder streams. Styles Brook and Clifford Brook are the only two tributaries big enough to contain fair populations of fish.

The West Branch has some larger tributaries that offer excellent fishing. Black Brook, which empties into the river just below the village of Wilmington, is large enough to fly-fish and produces a good population of fish. I've taken trout weighing up to 4 pounds from this brook. Other West Branch tributaries worth mentioning are Beaver Brook (excellent speckled trout fishing), Little Black Brook, Brown Brook, and White Brook. All of these tributaries are a mile or less from the village of Wilmington.

ACCOMMODATIONS

Those visiting this region for the first time will find several types of accommodations. In Wilmington, there are a number of reasonably priced motels. The West Branch Fly Fishing Club has its own motel where anglers can stay for a modest fee. It's located near the dam in town, right on the best fly-fishing section. The lodge has its own lounge with color TV and a large kitchen where fishermen can cook their own meals. Although members get first priority on the rooms, other fishermen are given the same rates when rooms are available. For anyone wishing up-to-date stream conditions on the West Branch, there is a local hot line that you can call from April 1 until October 15. That number is 518-946-2605.

A more upscale and generally more costly village to stay in is Lake Placid. This scenic site of past winter olympiads is admittedly a little bit glitzy, but it does offer a wide range of accommodations, and there are some very good restaurants. There is also good transportation in and out of Lake Placid.

Many out-of-town anglers who come to fish the Ausable choose a campground as an economical way to spend a few nights. There are a number of choices. One is the Wilmington Notch State Campground, which is located right in the middle of the fishiest section of the river. Another is Adirondack Lodge, which offers both indoor lodging and "primitive" outdoor camping. This is located just outside Lake Placid near the South Meadows area and is administered by the Adirondack Mountain

Club (ADK). Private campgrounds are also numerous in the Adirondacks and can be found in the various campground directories or through chambers of commerce.

The West Branch of the Ausable is a river worth traveling to, and indeed, some anglers travel thousands of miles to fish its productive waters. It offers all types of fishing conditions for anglers of all dispositions, from the timid to the most adventurous. In fact, many well-known anglers have fished these same waters over the years. Bergman's Run, just upstream of the Flume Pool, is named after Ray Bergman. Ray did much of his research for his book *Trout* here on the Ausable. He often fished this section of stream with my father, and I learned much of my fly-tying technique from this quiet and humble man. "Frustration Pool," located above the trophy section, was named by another good friend and fellow angler, Jim Deren. Jim never missed fishing his favorite pool on his yearly pilgrimages to the Ausable. He fished this pool for the last time only a few months before he passed away.

The scenic beauty of its tumbling currents in the shadow of Whiteface Mountain, its clean waters, and its abundance of trout make the West Branch of the Ausable a stream you will want to return to many times.

ABOUT THE AUTHOR

Francis Betters operates a large sporting goods business on the banks of the Ausable. He is a fly tyer of legend and has authored several now-famous patterns. He ties thousands of flies each year and holds free fly-fishing clinics and free barbecues throughout the summer. Call 518-946-2605 or check his website for dates at www.adirondackflyfishing.com. He has written 11 books on fishing and numerous magazine and newspaper articles. His latest book is a fly-fishing mystery novel set on the Ausable. Two new books are slated for release this season.

A beaver dam along one of the many small streams in the Tri-Lakes region.

CHAPTER SIX

In the Heart of the Adirondacks

BRIAN MCDONNELL

Deep, clear, and cold, Lake Placid lies in the heart of the mountains, at the eastern end of a chain of lakes extending west through the famous Saranac Lakes to scenic Tupper Lake. This so-called Tri-Lakes region of Essex and Franklin counties is a four-season angler's paradise. The large lakes covered in this chapter, together with numerous small ponds, rivers, and brooks in the area, present excellent opportunities for fishermen of every taste. Fly-fishing purists will be challenged by the land-locked salmon and trout populations, while worm anglers will enjoy the numerous species of panfish readily caught from boats, bridges, and shorelines.

LAKE PLACID

Located just outside the 1980 Winter Olympics host village, Lake Placid lies below Whiteface Mountain, the sixth highest of New York's high peaks. This spring-fed, glacial lake with a gravel- and boulder-strewn bottom and little vegetation, has an average depth of between 60 and 100 feet around its three prominent islands. It is ideal habitat for lake trout, brook trout (speckled trout), and rainbow trout, all of which are found here. There is also a healthy population of smallmouth bass.

According to Lake Placid fishing guide Captain Uwe Dramm, lake trout are best fished early in the spring at ice-out and again

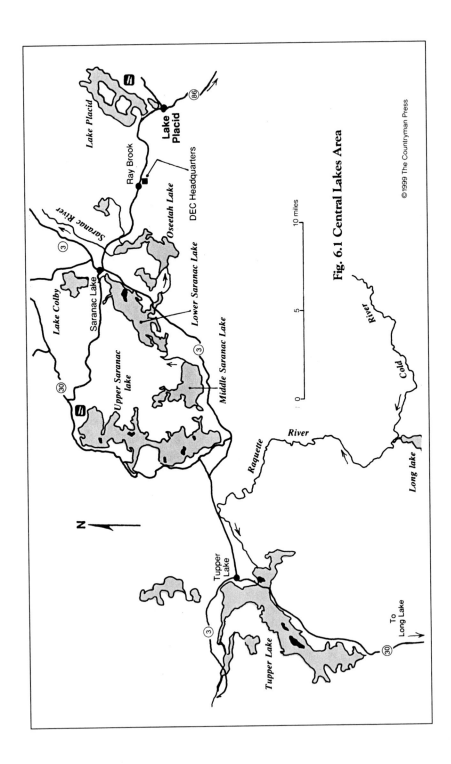

Fig. 6.1 Central Lakes Area

© 1999 The Countryman Press

in the fall. Slow trolling with spoons or spinners set well back on a flat line is best for surface fishing. Fifteen pounds or better is considered trophy size. An official state record lake trout was caught here in late spring of 1986. The lunker weighed 36 pounds, 8 ounces and was caught on a large spoon trolled slow.

Speckled trout are best fished after ice-out on light tackle when the water is still frigid. Small flies or fly-spinner combinations and other spinners or spoons produce results. Captain Dramm recommends that brook trout anglers use long leaders to successfully boat these easily spooked fish.

Rainbow trout are plentiful in Lake Placid, with many 5-pound-plus trophies available. While all of the trout species present reproduce naturally in the lake or its tributaries, New York State's Department of Environmental Conservation (DEC) annually supplements the wild rainbow population with an aggressive stocking program. Rainbow trout are best fished when the lake's surface water warms to more than 60 degrees Fahrenheit.

Lake Placid also supports a healthy smallmouth bass population. They are most common over rocky shoals, uprooted 100-foot white pines along shore, and man-made structures. Artificials, especially old-style wooden plugs and spinnerbaits, work well. Three-pound smallmouths are common. Trophy bass weighing as much as 6 pounds can also be found by the lucky and the skillful. Several large northern pike have come from the lake, including one 18-pounder caught a few years ago. Whitefish, too, are taken on occasion; they are native to Lake Placid but have been on the decline the past several decades. Sportsmen are encouraged to return whitefish to the lake unharmed. Because of the slow growth cycle of fish in the northern zone, anglers are encouraged to practice catch and release.

There are two excellent public boat launches with facilities near the village where lodging, meals, boat rentals, and bait are available.

TUPPER LAKE

Best known for its bass and pike fishing, Tupper Lake also offers quality lake trout and landlocked salmon fishing. The village of Tupper Lake has a long history of involvement in the wood products industry. The lake itself was dammed and enlarged to assist the transport of logs to the mill. The dams created numerous acres of shallow, weedy water and merged Raquette Pond with the main body of Tupper Lake. The expansive, shallow weed beds provide excellent habitat for northern pike, walleyes, and bass. Live bait is customarily used, though white and chartreuse spinnerbaits have grown in popularity in recent years.

The main body of the original lake stretches from Watch Island to the South Bay, where the Bog River (or Round Pond Outlet), empties into the lake in grand fashion over Bog River Falls. The numerous rocky islands and weedy shallow bays offer the bass angler a variety of fishing locations. Consistent, healthy catches have increased the popularity of the lake among both locals and visiting anglers.

Although Tupper Lake is best known for its warm-water species, anglers, taken with the scenery and pristine beauty of the lake, have discovered a well-kept "local secret"—lake trout and landlocked salmon. The deeper water between Norway Island and Black Point offers a challenging alternative to the normal Tupper Lake regimen. A word of caution: Your day of fishing is best planned for early morning or late afternoon as the prevailing winds blow up the lake on most days.

There is a state-maintained boat launch on Route 30 south of Tupper Lake village. Lodging, restaurants, boat rentals, and live bait are available in the village and around the lake.

See Frank Morrison's excellent little fishing guide to the Tupper Lake area. It is available at no cost from the Tupper Lake Chamber of Commerce at 518-359-3328.

LOWER SARANAC LAKE AND CONNECTED WATERS

Located just west of the village of Saranac Lake, the Saranac River connects Lower Saranac Lake to Middle Saranac Lake in the southwest and to Oseetah Lake, Kiwassa Lake, and Lake

Peaceful Saranac Lake on a misty morning.

Flower in the east. The state maintains two sets of locks to allow boat travel among these picturesque bodies of water. Fishermen can find tackle shops, live bait, groceries, and a wide variety of restaurants and accommodations for all tastes and budgets. Contact the Saranac Lake Area Chamber of Commerce, 30 Main Street, Saranac Lake, NY 12983 for more information. Campers can choose from among several area campgrounds or decide to take up residence on one of the many island campsites maintained by the DEC in Lower Saranac Lake. You will need a boat. Rentals are available at several locations around the lakes.

You can access the middle and lower lakes and the chain going into Saranac Lake village through the state-maintained boat ramps on either Lake Flower in Saranac Lake or at First Pond, by the state bridge 3 miles west of Saranac Lake on Route 3. There are several large private boat ramps, and the state maintains canoe and small boat launches at Ampersand Bay on

Lower Saranac Lake and on Route 3 at South Creek leading into Middle Saranac Lake.

The predominant sportfishing species in the chain of lakes leading from Lake Flower to Middle Saranac Lake are bass and northern pike. The numerous islands, expansive weed beds, and shallow, stumpy former farmlands created by the dam on Lake Flower provide excellent habitat and great fishing. Bass in the 1- to 3-pound range are common, while the occasional 5-pound-plus fish has been known to take a popping plug, golden shiner, spinnerbait, purple worm, or crayfish. Northern pike are vicious predators, thus a heavier weight line and a steel leader are recommended for best results. Pike are very opportunistic and often prey on wounded fish, so live bait or a lure resembling a perch or sucker are most effective. Northerns in the 3- to 5-pound range are common, while a 10-plus-pounder will give you all the fight you can handle.

There are numerous good fishing spots on each of the lakes. Concentrate on bass around the islands, rocky shoreline, and prominent structures like felled trees or docks in the early morning and evening. Locally known hot spots on Lower Saranac Lake include Ampersand Bay, Crescent Bay, and the Narrows. Pike can be found in the shallow, weedy bays almost anytime. Best bets are early mornings near the mouth of the Saranac River at the far end of the lake or evenings at the mouth of Fish Creek.

Lake Flower, near the village, is a popular fishing spot for both village residents and summer visitors. Bass and panfish are the primary catches. Oseetah Lake is shallow, stumpy, and loaded with weed beds. Northern pike are plentiful. You may have an opportunity to enjoy competing with an osprey, as they have been known to skim the surface, hook trophy size fish in their talons, and return to the top of an old dead pine for dinner.

Kiwassa Lake is tucked away up a channel east of Oseetah Lake. Good-sized pike are caught as they move up the waterway on their way to feed in the lake. The spring bass fishing here using popping plugs is excellent.

The Lower Lake is best known for bass, while the fisherman interested in northern pike will head for Middle Saranac (or

Round Lake, as it is known locally). Here, fishermen use spinnerbaits around the islands and tease the northerns out of the shallows of the western shoreline by trolling plugs behind a steel leader. A special place for lunch and good fishing hidden up a navigable waterway off the northern bay of Middle Saranac Lake is Weller Pond. In all of the lakes, the best fishing is in the spring and fall, but quality catches are at times enjoyed even on the hottest days of the summer.

Not to be overlooked in the Tri-Lakes area is ice fishing. The ice angler can enjoy some truly fine hard-water fishing in the area. One spot is in Lower Saranac Lake, where an angler can fill his bucket with the large numbers of smelt and yellow perch that winter in the shallow coves and weed beds of the lower lake.

LAKE COLBY AND UPPER SARANAC

Near Lower Saranac Lake, on Route 86, Lake Colby is another fine example of a year-round fisherman's paradise. In winter a virtual shanty town appears as ice fishermen establish themselves over their favorite holes. Species sought include rainbow and brown trout, as well as salmon, smelt, splake, and perch. The unofficial close of the ice-fishing season is the annual ice-fishing derby sponsored by the Saranac Lake Fish and Game Club held the first weekend of March. There are numerous cash and merchandise awards for winners in several categories.

When the ice goes out on Lake Colby, the fish shanties may disappear, but the fishermen do not. Canoe and small boat access is available at the DEC–maintained boat launch on Route 86 across from the General Hospital of Saranac Lake. Brown trout and splake are caught by patient springtime anglers trolling the length of the lake, from the beach to the state boat launch site and up the shore in front of DEC's Camp Colby Environmental Education Camp. Rainbows are sought by summertime fishermen trolling slowly around the middle of the lake, especially off the point past the former Camp Intermission. Bass fishermen have also discovered the shallows of the western bays of this year-round fishing hole.

Upper Saranac Lake is the largest in the chain, stretching 7 miles from the state-maintained boat ramp at the site of the historic Saranac Inn to the small boat launching site at the end of Indian Carry off Route 3. Some of the deepest water in the Adirondacks, 80–100 feet, is found in the area between Chapel Island and the Wawbeek Resort at the southern end of the lake. This deep water annually attracts lake trout fishermen to the upper lake, who anticipate the time when the lakers will be rolling on the water's surface and the chances will be best for landing a trophy fish. A second cold-water gamefish, the land-locked salmon, has also become popular among upper lake fishermen. Early June fly-rod trolling with lead core lines and large streamers is effective. As the summer weather forces the fish deeper, downriggers are useful in getting the lure to the fish.

The rocky, shallow coves and several large islands of Upper Saranac Lake offer anglers a complete change of tackle from that normally used for lakers or salmon. Smallmouth and rock bass are popular summertime species, as are northern pike in the shallow bays of the northern end of the lake. Live bait and spinnerbaits work best in Saginaw or Square Bays.

Adding to the diversity of the lake is the ice fishing that can be enjoyed for smelt and yellow perch on any of the bays accessible from Route 30 along the western shore of the lake.

Fishermen concentrating on the upper lake can find campsites, groceries, and supplies in Lake Clear or at Fish Creek on Route 30. Comfortable accommodations and meals are also available a short walk from the lake.

Another nighttime fishing activity popular with area residents and visiting campers is the pursuit of bullheads. Bullheads are a bottom-dwelling species present in every lake in the Saranac chain. Night crawlers, a bobber, a lamp, or fire, and a few good friends are all you need for a good night of bullheading.

The diverse opportunities for fishing in the Tri-Lakes and surrounding waterways provide the angler with numerous options within a half-hour drive of a motel room, campsite, or summer home. Cold-water species like lake trout, landlocked salmon, browns, rainbows, and splake; cool-water species like bass and northern pike; good-eating panfish like perch, rock bass, and sunfish; plus social fishing for bullheads in the spring and summer and smelt and perch in the winter—all this combines to make the Tri-Lakes Region a four-season fisherman's paradise.

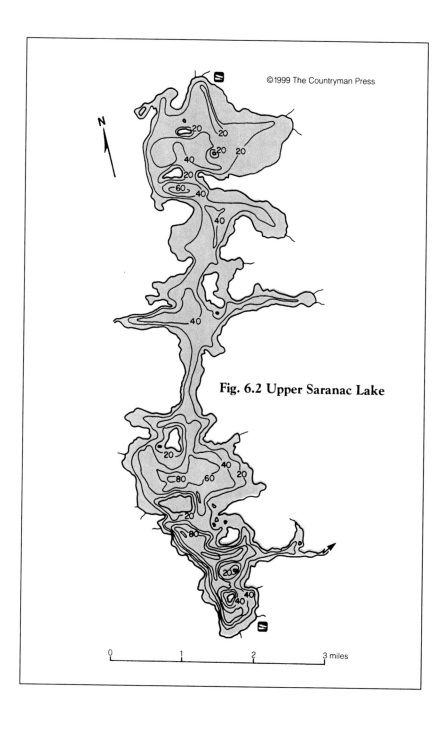

©1999 The Countryman Press

Fig. 6.2 Upper Saranac Lake

0   1   2   3 miles

ABOUT THE AUTHOR

Brian McDonnell is a New York State licensed guide, and is past president of the New York State Outdoor Guides association. He and his wife, Grace, operate McDonnell's Adirondack Challenges, a guide service, canoe livery, and camp store on Route 30 in Lake Clear. They lead fishing, canoeing, hiking, cross-country skiing, and snowshoeing trips in the Adirondacks.

CHAPTER SEVEN

Backcountry Fishing Trips

DENNIS APRILL

Back in the 1880s, hiking into a remote Adirondack pond either with or without a guide and guideboat to fish for native brook trout with a cane fly-rod was considered by many anglers to be the ultimate experience. That experience is still possible today. Granted, there may not be many remote ponds that hold 5-pound brookies, but there are still plenty of backcountry streams and small lakes that are stocked and offer excellent fishing. These are spread throughout the Adirondack Park, but be aware that in many of the ponds above 2,000 feet in the western Adirondacks, fish populations have been wiped out by acid precipitation. So, the focus of this chapter will be on the Adirondack heartland, and on one trail in particular—the Northville–Lake Placid (N–P) Trail—that cuts through the center of the Park, providing access to some great fishing.

The N–P Trail is a winding 120-mile thoroughfare made by the Adirondack Mountain Club in 1922. Its original southern terminus was the Sacandaga River bridge in Northville. Today, most hikers start at Benson, 13 miles to the north. Sections of the N–P Trail are perfect for anglers, because the winding path follows the valleys and climbs only the passes. It hugs many watersheds that hold trout.

Following is a selection of backcountry fishing opportunities along the N–P. For a detailed description of the trail, call

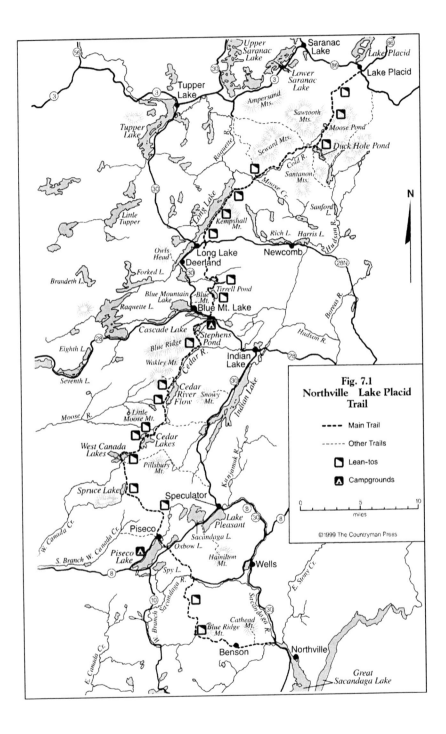

Fig. 7.1
Northville — Lake Placid Trail

- – – – Main Trail
- - - - - Other Trails
- 🏠 Lean-tos
- 🔺 Campgrounds

```
0          5          10
        miles
```

©1999 The Countryman Press

N

for a copy of the Adirondack Mountain Club's *Guide to the Northville–Lake Placid Trail* (1-800-395-8080).

LAKE PLACID–DUCK HOLE POND

Duck Hole Pond sits south of Lake Placid, 9.4 miles from the N–P trailhead off the Averyville Road. The parking area is on the right, just beyond the Chubb River and the yellow-on-brown Department of Environmental Conservation (DEC) trail marker.

The hike into Duck Hole should be planned as an overnight. There are lean-tos at the pond, but they are often filled, so plan on bringing along a lightweight tent in addition to a sleeping bag, cook kit, and other camping gear. A four-section spinning or fly-rod packs well. Also bring along an assortment of flies, such as Mickey Finns, Hornbergs, Woolly Buggers, Royal Wulffs, or Adams in sizes 8–12. For spinning rigs, smaller spoons such as Little Cleos, Panther Martins, or spinners like those made by Mepps work well.

Sections of the trail into Duck Hole parallel the Chubb River, a narrow stream lined with large tamaracks. The Chubb is stocked with brown trout and also holds some brook trout. Pause along the way to do some fishing. The water just below Wanika Falls, some 4 miles from the trailhead, is especially worth a stop.

Duck Hole is stocked by air with 2,800 brook trout each spring. Besides the usual spinning lures and dry flies, worms are great fish producers here. You won't need a fancy rig, just some small splitshot, or better yet, let the worm sink naturally without added weight.

DAY TRIP SOUTH OF LAKE DURANT

From the trailhead at the Lake Durant Campground off Route 28/30, 3 miles east of Blue Mountain Lake, the N–P goes south, reaching Stephens Pond at 2½ miles. Stephens is stocked annually with 1,300 brown trout and can easily be fished from the shoreline.

One mile west of Stephens is Cascade Pond, a small pond that is stocked by air with 2,400 brook trout. Cascade can be reached by a marked side trail that heads northwest of Stephens Pond.

From Cascade Pond, the trail goes west, then north to Lake Durant (a cool-water fishery stocked with tiger muskellunge) and Route 28/30. The 1-mile walk back to the parking area at the campground is on hardtop highway. Alternatively, you can leave another vehicle at the roadside near the cemetery off 28/30, ¾ of a mile east of Blue Mountain Lake Village.

PISECO NORTH

The N–P Trail north of Piseco Lake is the gateway to the remote West Canada Lake Wilderness and some of the best brook trout fishing in the Adirondacks. From Piseco village, the N–P goes north for 3 miles, then veers northwest, crossing the Jessup River after 7½ miles and arriving at Spruce Lake in 10 miles. Spruce is stocked by air with over 5,000 brook trout. There are three lean-tos at this lake for overnight camping.

From Spruce, the N–P continues north 6 miles into the heart of the Wilderness area and to three major brook trout lakes: West Canada lake, South Lake, and Mud Lake. All of these waters are stocked with brook trout. West Canada Creek, the outlet, is also an excellent brook trout water, but some bush-whacking is required to reach the brook's headwaters.

Each of the three lakes has a lean-to nearby (West Canada has two), but be prepared to camp out, as this area is popular during July and August, probably the slowest months for brook trout fishing. For serious anglers, early May and late September are the best times to fish for brookies. During these times, you'll also find fewer people and almost no blackflies, the scourge of the Adirondacks in late May and early June.

TRIP POINTERS

For overnights, try to keep your pack weight in the 30-pound range. Bring along a tent in case lean-tos are full, but remember that no camping is allowed within 150 feet of water. Be sure to follow the number one rule of camping etiquette: Carry out what you bring in. Stow food safely with cable or rope sus-

This hiker fishes a remote Adirondack pond for brook trout. Solitude and a chance to catch wild native brook trout are reasons why many like to backpack in with their fishing gear.

pended from a tree limb so as not to attract bears. Finally, practice catch and release, or keep only the fish you intend to eat that day.

EXOTIC FISHING TRIPS— ADIRONDACK STYLE

FLY-OUT FISHING

As the pontooned Cessna taxied down Long Lake to get into position for takeoff, I got a strange feeling of déjà vu: For an instant that June day in 1992, I thought I was back in northern Canada, where for years I had flown into remote lakes in search of trout. Even after we took off, the scenery—thick softwood forests, open bogs, and sparkling lakes—all looked strikingly similar to northern Ontario. Our destination was Upper Sargent Lake, 10 miles to the southwest.

My pilot, Herb Helms, had been flying out anglers, hunters, and campers since 1947, and although Helms told me at the time

A proud angler with a Kokance salmon caught in Polliwog Pond, St. Regis Canoe Area. He sits in a small, easily transported rowing canoe.

it's not like the "old days" when he could land on 40 or more Adirondack lakes, there are still a dozen or so that are still open to float planes. Many of these lakes are excellent fish producers.

After we landed on Upper Sargent, Herb taxied over to a large island midway down the lake, one of two good camping areas. There was also a nice campsite on a second, smaller island farther down the lake.

While we disembarked, Herb talked about fishing. Because it was midsummer, most of the trout fishing had slowed to a standstill in Pine and Lower Sargent, two of Helms's better-producing trout lakes. Brook trout as large as 4 pounds have been taken in both (not frequently though), but these lakes peak in midspring and early fall. For those going after trout, a canoe is a necessity (bring your own or rent one in Long Lake village). The usual assortment of lures and baits that work elsewhere in northern New York will take trout in Pine and Lower Sargent. Still a popular choice, the Lake Clear Wabbler trolled slowly with 8 inches of line and a worm on a hook is great for trout. Other trout ponds that can be reached by float plane include Tirrell and Trout Ponds, Lower Squaw, and First Lakes; the last also contains some nice rainbows and lake trout.

Fishing for cool-water species like perch, which are plentiful in Upper Sargent, and bass obviously requires a different approach, but once again, a canoe will make fishing that much easier. For perch, the common earthworm always seems to work. Find a school of these panfish, drop in a worm, and your chances of catching a nice mess of these excellent eating fish are good. Another technique that works well on Upper Sargent is slowly trolling with a floating Rapala through the weeds.

Most pilots can transport as much as 250 pounds of gear plus two anglers, who have to supply their own food and camping equipment. The normal fly-out trip lasts from 3–5 days, and an extra day or two supply of food is recommended just in case the pilot can't get in because of bad weather. Parties staying more than 3 nights must get a camping permit (obtained by contacting the local forest ranger).

When it came time for us to leave Upper Sargent, the cry of a loon in the south bay mingled with the aircraft propeller, and once again I had that feeling of "being there" before. Fly-out fishing is not for those in a hurry, but rather for people who want to relax and have a quality wilderness experience, whether they catch a boatload of fish or not. Herb Helms passed away in 1998, but there are a number of fly-out pilots in Long Lake village, inlet, and other areas throughout the Adirondacks. Contact area chambers of commerce for a list.

ADVENTURE ON PACKHORSE

Just the thought of sitting on a horse for 14 miles gave me a pain in the rear. But, after being reassured by John Fontana, owner of Cold River Ranch, that his horses were quite gentle, I felt a little more at ease. "Confidence," said Fontana, "is the main ingredient a person needs for a successful packhorse trip; no experience is necessary."

On a ranch harboring 17 horses of mixed breeds, Cold River leads packhorse trips into the mountains throughout the spring, summer, and fall from Coreys, west of Tupper Lake. Trip length varies from 1 to 3 days, as do destinations. Anglers usually go to Raquette Falls or farther west to the Cold River region and remote ponds higher in the mountains.

Most packhorse outfitters use true western-style accommodations with cook tents, complete with table and stove and wall tents for sleeping. With packhorses, there are really no weight problems, and most outfitters provide the camping equipment. Anglers need only bring fishing gear and personal luxuries. In the case of Cold River Ranch, riders travel along the state horse-trail system, which weaves in and out of the Steward and Santanoni Mountains.

For packhorse trips, a collapsible pole, lightweight spinning reel, and spinners like Panther Martins, Roostertails, and Mepps or an assortment of trout flies work well.

Information about packhorse outfitters can be had from the nearest area chambers of commerce and tourism agencies.

RAFTING FOR WHITEWATER TROUT

By the time we floated through the second series of haystacks, I finally began to ease up on the rope tied securely to the raft's outer shell. We were rapidly approaching the juncture where

A rafter fishes in the Hudson River near Blue Ledges in Hudson Gorge. This stretch of the river holds some sizeable brown and rainbow trout.

the Indian River joins up with the Hudson River. The main thrust of "the bubble," that initial gust from the water release at Lake Abanakee, had passed us by, so we could now float toward our intended campsite at Blue Ledges. The "we" referred to here were three fishermen from the New York City area, myself, and Wayne Failing, our guide. It was late September 1991.

Failing, owner of Middle Earth Expeditions out of Lake Placid, has run rafting trips for 20 years and is probably the most seasoned whitewater guide on the upper Hudson. This was reassuring, because when he first invited me along, my initial response was: "What class are the rapids?"

"They'll be about class III, with waves only 4 feet high," Failing replied. Having never been whitewater rafting, I envisioned an experience akin to riding the Screamin Demon at Great Escape near Glens Falls. This was not the case.

In fact, from the confluence with the Hudson, we began casting into the eddies and holes along the cedar ledges for rainbows and browns. We used the usual assortment of spinning baits like Mepps, Abu Reflexes, Roostertails, and Panther Martins of various sizes. Unfortunately, the rainbows weren't biting, so we focused on the browns, catching and releasing some nice-sized fish.

We were the last ones out of the launch site below Lake Abanakee, so thankfully, we were left to float behind the throng of rafts that congregate on the river weekends throughout the spring, summer, and fall.

By early afternoon, we had arrived at Blue Ledges, and while Failing set up camp, we fished the rocky shoreline. Luckily, that last weekend in September was a cool one, and most of the campsites at Blue Ledges were empty; as a result, there was little fishing pressure. I took out my old favorite for brown trout, a 4-inch silver Rapala, and worked the slower stretches. Two of the other fellows fanned out downstream, and one who had never caught a freshwater fish before cast in a pool in front of our campsite. As luck would have it, he caught the largest fish of the trip—a 16-inch brown trout weighing 2 pounds.

The next day, Sunday, after fishing the early morning hours, we once again caught "the bubble" down the Hudson. As we slithered through the Osprey Nest Rapids, Given's Rift, and the Black Hole, we were treated to 360s around rocks, and when there was a shore audience, a few "shake and bake" moves through drop-offs.

From where the Hudson flows under the Delaware and Hudson railroad bridge to North River, trip's end, there are ample fishing opportunities, especially where the Boreas River joins the Hudson.

Failing runs rafting/fishing trips throughout the spring and fall when the town of Indian Lake allows water releases from Abanakee Dam. In the spring, I am told, with class V rapids, things can get a little hairy. Middle Earth Expeditions can be reached at 518-523-9572.

ABOUT THE AUTHOR

Dennis Aprill is editor of *Good Fishing in the Adirondacks*.

CHAPTER EIGHT

The Peaceful Schroon Lake Area

VAL DE CESARE
UPDATED BY VAL DE CESARE, HIS SON

Cradled at the foot of Pharaoh Mountain is a 9-mile lake that offers visitors a panoramic view of the Adirondack Mountains. Schroon Lake begins at a point some 5 miles north of Chestertown and extends to 1 mile north of Schroon Lake village. Schroon is a very pretty lake with deep blue waters. It has a surface area of 4,230 acres and a maximum depth of 152 feet. Although it is about 9 miles long, the lake's widest point, off Adirondack village at the southern end, is only about 1½ miles. The lake's north–south axis parallels US Route 9 between Exits 26 and 28 of the Northway. Northbound motorists should get off at Exit 26 from I-87 and head north on Route 9; those southbound should use Exit 28 and head south on Route 9.

There are two public boat launches on Schroon Lake. One is in the village of Schroon Lake and is free. The other is in the town of Horicon at the southern tip of Schroon Lake. This is a state-owned boat launch site and is also free. There is a marina at the northern tip of the lake that will accommodate all of your boating needs. You may also moor your boat there between fishing trips. Year-round fishing is permitted for most species, though northern pike is closed between March 15 and May 1.

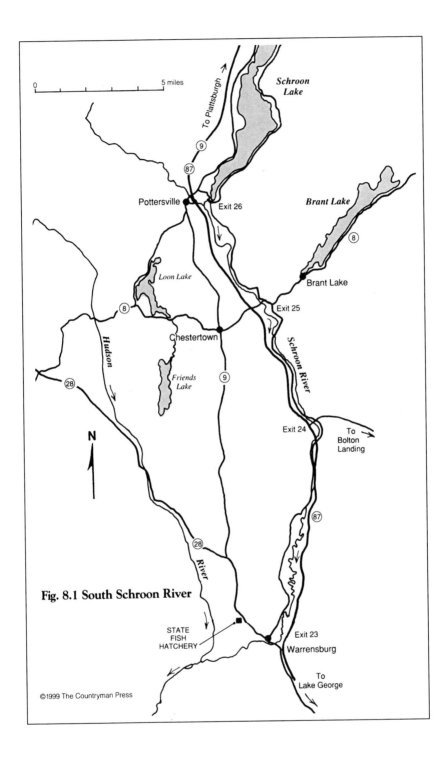

Fig. 8.1 South Schroon River

©1999 The Countryman Press

FISHING TIPS

Schroon Lake is noted for its landlocked salmon and has always supported a natural population of this species. Lately, the Department of Environmental Conservation has been conducting an intensive program to bolster salmon numbers. The best time to fish for landlocks is early spring when the fish are near or at the surface feeding on the smelt that congregate near the mouths of streams at this time.

In the spring, I prefer to fish with a small boat and motor, trolling the areas out from the mouth of the Schroon River or other small tributaries. The most popular locations are the entire north end of the lake above Sola Bella Island and south of the Schroon River. During periods of high water, this whole portion may be trolled, including the river itself. Water depth may restrict you at other times.

Most of the local fishermen prefer to troll streamer flies, Rapalas, and Mooselook Wabblers. Rapalas should be trolled at about 3½ miles per hour; Mooselooks are trolled between 3½ and 4½ miles per hour. Streamer flies are trolled rather fast, and they must be jerked periodically to give them a fishlike appearance as they are pulled through the water.

The Sebago Smelt and the Grey Ghost are probably the most-used streamer patterns. Other colors and patterns may be used, but you must remember that you are trying to imitate smelt. A number 7 Rapala in either silver or gold is my favorite. Give the Countdown Rapala a try when the surface water is extremely cold. This lure trolls a little deeper and may help you connect. My favorite colors for Mooselooks are white/red dots and orange/black dots.

Summer fishing for landlocks is a completely different story. The lures, for the most part, must be kept at or near the thermocline. This requires more sophisticated equipment, and hiring a guide might be the best strategy for a novice. Those having the proper equipment may use the same lures and speeds recommended for spring surface trolling. Downriggers are the most efficient way of getting your lure to the thermocline, but you may use lead core line too. You'll have to experiment with just how much line to let out. The weight of your line and the speed at which you move will determine how deep your

Nice Catch! Ice fishing is very popular on Schroon Lake throughout the winter.

lure runs. A good place to start would be in the 18- to 25-foot range.

Trolling for lake trout probably is best from late May to the middle of July. Techniques for lake trout differ greatly from those used for landlocked salmon, though. Trolling along the bottom and at slower speeds is recommended. Some people prefer copper trolling line to bring their lure to the bottom, while others prefer lead core line or steel line with or without a sinker to hold bottom. Lures for lake trout include those used for salmon plus many other local favorites, like Skinny Hinckleys, Suttons, and Leatherstockings, to name a few. It has traditionally been best to troll in water that is 30–80 feet deep. (Very few fish are ever caught in water deeper than 80 feet.) I prefer water that is between 40 and 80 feet deep.

Lake trout get very lazy as the summer progresses. Reducing your trolling speed will sometimes produce some action. A streamer fly or live bait behind a Lake Clear Wabbler will entice even the laziest big guys. I prefer 1–1.5 miles per hour when the hot summer sun really warms the lake.

One of the local favorite spots to fish lake trout is the area immediately west of Sola Bella Island, also known as Clark's Island and Word of Life Island. Troll north–south about 200 yards west of the island, principally covering the southern half. Then head from the southern tip of the island west toward Grove Point. Another favorite spot for forktails is the easterly shore of the narrows. This water is approximately 60–80 feet deep.

Probably the most productive area for lunker lakers is in the southern half of the lake. There is a sunken island between Adirondack village and Scaroon Manor that is always well marked with buoys. Try all around this spot, especially where the water is 50–80 feet deep (which is primarily north and west of Sunken Island). There is an 8-foot channel that runs north–south between Scaroon Manor and Eagle Point. Fish the shallower portions of this channel early in the year, and then go deeper as the water warms.

Another good laker spot runs from Adirondack village north toward the Narrows. This area is very uneven in depth and not very well defined as to direction. If you want, just try to hold to about a 50-foot depth. Don't worry if your depth varies. Going south from Adirondack village along the east shore, I would hold between 50 and 80 feet.

In the fall, as the surface temperature drops to approximately 55 degrees, salmon and lake trout may again be caught on the surface. Use the same techniques and lures as for spring fishing for these species.

ICE FISHING

Fishing through the ice is probably the most effective way to land lunker lake trout and salmon. Schroon Lake and most of the surrounding ponds freeze up solid by about December 20, give or take 10 days.

Fowler Avenue and Dock Street provide the ice fisherman with two excellent access points to the northern portion of Schroon Lake. Just out from Fowler Avenue on the west shore is a good drop-off for lakers and salmon. Dock Street usually provides good vehicular access to the whole northern basin. Again, the area west of the island is excellent. Another good spot is the eastern shore below the island. Shanties are usually very much in evidence over the better locations. The central portion of the lake is probably best in the general vicinity of the Narrows. Access to this area can be made via Hayes Road off Route 9, or over the bank by the Narrows Restaurant.

About a mile south of Exit 27 (northbound only) off I-87 is Eagle Point Campsite. Just north and south of the campsite along the eastern shoreline is another good area to fish. Access is obtained through the campsite or by parking farther south and walking out onto the lake.

Continuing south along Route 9 and just north of the town of Pottersville, we take a right onto River Road. Cross the Schroon River bridge and pass the state boat launch at Horicon, then go left onto East Shore Road. Approximately 4 miles to the north, you will see the village of Adirondack, where Mill Brook enters Schroon Lake. This is a good access point to fish the east shore of the southern basin. Fish fairly close to shore to the south, and go farther away from shore to the north. Again, there should be some shanties out to guide you.

Live smelt suspended about 10–15 feet below the ice seem to produce the most fish, but dead smelt are sometimes just as effective. (Smelt may be purchased at the local bait stores.) I like to stay in waters that are between 30 and 60 feet deep, but I have seen fish caught in waters up to 80 and 100 feet deep. If smelt are unavailable, suckers or shiners may do the trick.

Each fisherman is allowed five tip-ups and two hand lines. Bait, tackle, and licenses are available in Schroon Lake, South Schroon, and Pottersville.

A key to success in most of these Adirondack lakes is light tackle. Small hooks in the 6–10 range and 4- to 8-pound-test line will greatly increase your success. Most of my catches have come on minnows less than 3 inches long. Always maintain your tip-up holes. Keeping your equipment free from ice will certainly help.

There are many food establishments open in Schroon Lake for winter fishermen, but motel accommodations are more limited, and advance reservations are recommended.

COOL-WATER SPECIES

While landlocks and lakers provide much action here, there are many other fish present in Schroon Lake. These include smallmouth and largemouth bass, northern pike, yellow perch, smelt, calico bass, rock bass, sunfish, suckers, and various minnows.

Smallmouth bass prefer rocky shelves and shoals. Largemouth bass (not very abundant) prefer weedy portions of shallows. A few good bass spots are as follows: in the north basin, in the bay directly opposite Fowler Avenue on the east shore; around a rock pile just north of the public beach in Schroon Lake village and a good mess of rocks running westerly off the southern tip of the island (this bunch of rocks runs about halfway across the lake and then drops off into 80 feet of water); by a big rock shelf off the Narrows Restaurant (this runs from the east shore about halfway across the lake); and around the Sunken Island in the south basin. Remember one thing: The shallower areas around these shoals are excellent habitat for the cool-water species such as bass, perch, pike, and panfish, while the deeper areas are excellent habitat for trout and salmon.

PARADOX LAKE

About 3 miles northeast of Schroon Lake lies Paradox Lake. This lake derives its name from an old Indian word that means "flowing backwards." During the spring, when the thaw is at its peak, the Schroon River (and its Paradox Creek tributary) actually reverses its flow back into Paradox Lake. For a short time, Paradox Lake has no outlet.

Five-mile-long Paradox Lake has a maximum depth of 52 feet and a surface area of 860 acres. It is divided into two halves, with a narrow, streamlike portion dividing the two sections. The eastern sector has a maximum depth of 27 feet. It is the home of most of the cool-water species of fish that reside in Paradox.

To get to Paradox Lake, take Route 87 to Exit 28, then go east along Route 74 about 1 mile. There is a public boat launch at the state campsite located about 3 miles farther along Route 74. There is a fee for parking. Most of your supplies should be bought in advance.

Paradox Lake has lake trout, a few landlocked salmon, rainbow trout, smallmouth and largemouth bass, great northern pike, pickerel, lake herring, bullheads, perch, calico bass, and numerous other panfish. Rainbow trout and all of the cool-water fish are spread throughout the lake. The lake trout here are concentrated primarily in the western sector. Trolling for lake trout is done much the same as it is in Schroon Lake. Most of the productive waters are around the rim of the 52-foot depth. The inlet to Paradox Lake lies at its easternmost end. There are mostly weed beds and shallow shelves near here. These make for good winter fishing for perch. Winter perch are among the best fish for eating.

The outlet of Paradox begins at the westernmost end of the lake and flows (except in spring as noted) until it enters Schroon River just south of Route 74. This is a slow-flowing stream and has been known to produce some good-sized brown trout. Of course, you have to get back off the main road and be there in late spring or early summer.

Paradox Lake has produced lake trout in the 16- to 20-pound class, rainbow trout up to 8 pounds, largemouth bass more than 6 pounds, and northern pike more than 24 pounds. There are some tackle busters in there yet that will beat these.

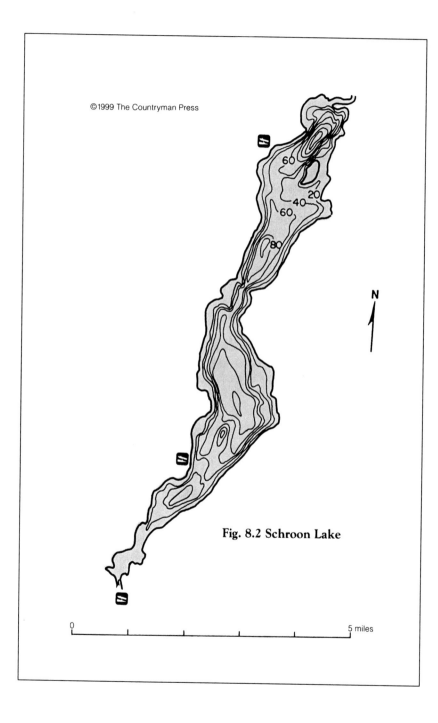

60

20

40

60

80

N

Fig. 8.2 Schroon Lake

0   5 miles

The prime lake trout area in Paradox Lake is at the western end of the lake. It resembles a triangle that begins at the western end of the narrows (Brier Point), carrying due west to a point jutting out into the lake from the western end of Grovesnor Bay, then due south to a boat house, then easterly back to Brier Point. The maximum depth of this triangle is 52 feet with just a few variations. Using the same trolling methods recommended for Schroon Lake, you should troll all around this triangle. Some of the time you should hit it a little higher on the shoulders. This applies in summer and winter.

Largemouth bass and northern pike are caught in the weedy sections in the easternmost part of the lake and in the narrows. Fishing through the ice at Smiths Bay (Nawita Bay) has produced some lunker pike. Pike weighing 22–24 pounds have been caught there in each of the past four or five winters.

Perch can be caught in almost every corner of the lake. Fishing for perch in the winter is a favorite pastime for local anglers. Most of it is done on the eastern end of the lake and in Nawita Bay.

Smallmouth bass can be caught at either end of the lake. Fish for them off the rocky ledges with surface lures cast from a boat just before and after dark. Any of your favorites should work here. You can troll for rainbow trout at either end of the lake. Most of the fishermen use a set of spinners with a trailing night crawler. Troll the lure about 10–15 feet down.

THE SCHROON RIVER

The portion of the Schroon River that flows into Schroon Lake will be the only part of the river discussed here. It begins at a point just south of Exit 30 of the Northway and flows south for about 17 miles before entering the lake. This 17 miles would be as the crow flies—the river actually zigs and zags along its way for probably 40 miles or more.

Several miles south of Exit 30, the river first crosses Route 9 from east to west. This is known as Deadwater Bridge. This, for all practical purposes, is the beginning of the northern portion of the Schroon River. About a mile south of Deadwater Bridge, the river crosses Route 9 again, this time from west to east.

There is a public campsite at this crossing (Sharp's Bridge Campsite). Between Deadwater Bridge and Sharp's Bridge, Lindsey Brook enters the Schroon River. Almost exactly 0.5 mile farther south along Route 9, there is a small trail that turns right down a slight hill. This is the road that leads to West Mill Brook. It is a wilderness road, traversable by most but not all vehicles. Greenough Road is another access point to the Schroon River. It lies just about 2 miles below the Sharp's Bridge Campsite.

The section between Sharp's Bridge and Greenough Road winds away from any roads for about 2 miles. This is one of the best runs on the Schroon River, and it's a good place to spend a day.

Just about a mile south of Greenough Road is Pepper Hollow Road. By taking a right on this road, you will first cross West Mill Brook, then you will meet the Schroon River again. The river parallels the road along its full length. The river is now west of Route 9 and will not cross again until Schroon River Falls, which is about 9 miles farther south. Between Pepper Hollow Road and Schroon River Falls, the river parallels Route 9 and I-87 and is never very far from either. The section of the Schroon River below Pepper Hollow Road and Black Brook Road (the Port Henry Road) is another section of the river that can be very productive for both brook and brown trout. In between there is one other road crossing at Frontier Town in the hamlet of North Hudson. This is where the Branch, a tributary flowing east from the Blue Ridge, also joins the Schroon River.

This entire section of the Schroon watershed is well stocked with brook trout and brown trout. There are trout in all the tributaries as well. The Branch is almost entirely posted by private clubs, and permission to fish it is difficult but possible to obtain. Again it should be emphasized that the better fishing would be away from the roads and beaten paths.

The stretch above North Hudson is primarily small-stream fishing. Here it is probably best to fish the old-fashioned way— by wading the stream. A flat-bottom boat or a shallow-running canoe may be used in some sections, but it will be necessary to get out and portage around many obstacles and sandbars. Speckled trout weighing a pound or better have been caught in this section

Ice fishing is extremely popular on Schroon Lake. Northern pike is only one of several species that make braving the cold worthwhile.

of the Schroon, but be careful in identifying trout. Young salmon are at times very plentiful in this sector. Please be careful in releasing them.

Below North Hudson, the Schroon River becomes larger and lazier. It meanders its way south and has very little fast water. This is a very good section to fly-fish for some sassy brown trout. Fall fly-fishing this section has also produced some healthy acrobatic salmon. Even lake trout and pike have been caught this far north during the sucker spawning runs in the spring right after ice-out. This section is best handled by floating a small flat-bottom boat or a canoe. There are no major obstacles to the falls at Route 9.

Spring fishing for salmon and lake trout is very good in late April and early May in the Schroon River just above where it enters the lake. Trolling a Grey Ghost or other smelt imitation or a small floating Rapala works very well. Once you tangle with a 3-pound or larger salmon in the river, you will be hooked for life.

TROUT BROOK

Trout Brook is a beautiful stream of pure mountain waters. It lies about 6 miles to the west of Schroon Lake, flows from north to south parallel to the lake, then turns east to join the Schroon River below the lake. Trout Brook begins in the Hoffman Notch Wilderness area, then flows south toward Olmsteadville. It is well stocked with speckled trout, and there is a head of naturally bred trout in the upper reaches and tributaries. If you ever had the desire to taste a meal of freshly caught native brook trout, this is the stream to fish. It is posted in many locations, but permission to cross private lands may sometimes be obtained via a polite request. The best fishing opportunities lie in the upper reaches, where the fish are small but wonderfully good to eat.

To get to this brook, take the Hoffman Road, which is located just south of Schroon Lake village on Route 9. Go west for about 6 miles to what is known as Olmsteadville Road. Just before hitting this road, you will cross a small stream. This is Trout Brook. Topographic maps will show some access spots north of this point. (There aren't any road crossings above here.) Turning south, you will cross the brook in several spots. South of the next bridge takes you into an area of slow-moving water and many beaver dams. This is a good section to fish from a canoe or flat-bottom boat.

OTHER NEARBY ADIRONDACK WATERS

Probably the most beautiful and bountiful fisheries in the area are the vast number of backwoods ponds. Crane Pond and Goose Pond are easily accessed via Crane Pond Road off Schroon's East Shore Road and Alder Meadow Road. Goose Pond is about a ¾-mile hike. The pond is well stocked with brookies and splake, as well as other trout species. Crane Pond is accessible with a car, so fishermen with limited mobility can give this pond a try. Crane Pond is also stocked with several trout species as well as cool-water fish species.

The waters and wetlands of the Schroon drainage, like all those in the Adirondack Forest Preserve, are of extraordinary value. They support a wide range of wildlife. They are also natural recreation areas affording unlimited opportunities for bird-watching, wildlife observation, photography, and canoeing as well as fishing, hunting, and trapping. Please use the utmost care when visiting all these wild areas. Carry out what you carry in, and don't bury anything unless it is readily biodegradable. Make sure all fires are out before you leave camp.

The Schroon Lake region is one of the most beautiful in New York State. If visitors use it wisely, it can remain so.

ABOUT THE AUTHORS

The late Val De Cesare was an avid fisherman and outdoorsman who lived in the Schroon Lake area. He knew the Schroon watershed and myriad surrounding waters as well as anyone. His son Val continues his father's tradition, fishing the Schroon area 30 weeks each year.

CHAPTER NINE

Lake George

ROBERT ZAJAC, WITH RICKY DOYLE

In the summer of 1642, a French Jesuit priest named Father Jogues became the first white man to witness the picturesque beauty and crystal clear waters of Lake George. He had traveled south from Canada via the Richelieu River and Lake Champlain. Upon reaching the great body of water, he named it Lake of the Holy Sacrament. As a missionary, his purpose was to convert the Iroquois to Christianity. Unfortunately, his arrival coincided with an epidemic among the Iroquois, which they blamed on the French clergy. Father Jogues was subjected to numerous tortures and was eventually beheaded with the blow of a tomahawk. Thus the "Mission of the Martyrs" was sealed with the blood of the lake's European discoverer.

Few lakes in our country can rival either the scenic grandeur or the historical significance of Lake George. Its present name was given by Sir William Johnson, who in 1754 led his militia north while the colonies were still under the rule of King George II. In literature, James Fenimore Cooper's legendary fictional characters from *The Last of the Mohicans*—Hawkeye, Chingachgook, and Uncas—came from Leatherstocking country to fight near Fort William Henry. Fort Ticonderoga on Lake Champlain, located at the foot of Lachute Rapids (the natural outlet for Lake George), was the keystone of control for the most important north–south waterway in the colonies. In the latter half of the 18th century, this region was the violent setting

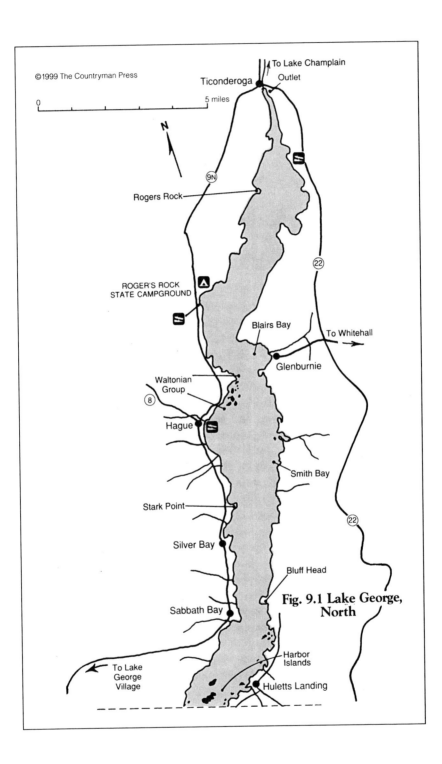

To Lake Champlain

Ticonderoga
Outlet

0   5 miles

N

9N

Rogers Rock

22

ROGER'S ROCK
STATE CAMPGROUND

Blairs Bay

To Whitehall

Glenburnie

Waltonian
Group

8

Hague

Smith Bay

Stark Point

22

Silver Bay

Bluff Head

**Fig. 9.1 Lake George,
North**

Sabbath Bay

To Lake
George
Village

Harbor
Islands

Huletts Landing

for numerous contests as France and England fought for control of the continent. Visiting anglers who are also history buffs should expand their itineraries to include visits to Fort Ticonderoga, Fort William Henry, and Crown Point.

OVERVIEW

Lake George, sometimes called America's most beautiful lake, is a product of the late Pleistocene epoch, also known as the great Ice Age. It was formed by the scouring retreat of a great glacier that left natural dams on its north and south ends. Runoff from the Adirondacks to the west and the Green Mountains to the east feed its 32-mile length. Rarely more than a mile and a half wide, with a notable maximum depth of 201 feet, the lake offers 28,200 acres of premier fishing. It is easily reached from the Northway (I-87), and Exits 20 through 28 will bring you to the lake with its 365 islands. Yes, one island for each day of the year!

The New York State Department of Environmental Conservation (DEC) maintains 47 islands for overnight camping by permit only. This allows fishermen to have rods in the water even while the breakfast bacon is frying. An additional 11 islands are maintained for day use only (no permit required) and can provide the scenic setting for a tasty shore lunch. DEC has a separate listing for camping information in the Lake George telephone directory, and a quick phone call will provide you with all the necessary details as well as their brochure.

The narrows divides Lake George in two, and the halves are known locally as the North Basin and the South Basin, each holding its own secrets. Like Lake Champlain, Lake George is another two-story fishery of impressive dimension. It offers cool-water fishing for largemouth bass, smallmouth bass, northern pike, pickerel, and panfish (mainly perch and crappies), as well as good opportunities for its cold-water residents, landlocked salmon and lake trout.

BASS FISHING

Bass season opens the third Saturday in June and closes on November 30. Fishing for largemouth and smallmouth bass can be great throughout the summer months.

From opening day until mid-July, the largemouths can be found fairly shallow in the many bays, such as Weeds, Blairs, Dark, Gull, and Indian in the North Basin and Huddle, Boon, Warren, Harris, and Dunham in the South Basin. During this time of the year, these fish can be caught around docks, around submerged wood, and in milfoil in the backs of the bays. Lures of choice in these situations would be ¼- to ½-ounce black and blue jigs with plastic or pork trailers. Another good choice would be a 4- or 6-inch black or red shad plastic worm. Top-water baits such as the Zaraspook, the Sluggo, or the Pop-R are all excellent choices when you wish to cover a lot of water while looking for active fish. As the water warms in mid-July, the large-mouth bass head for deeper waters, in the 20–25 feet range. These fish can also be caught on a regular basis, but it takes a totally different technique: Carolina rigging. To Carolina rig, you use a ¾-ounce egg sinker, a plastic bead, a barrel swivel, and a 3-foot leader. The hook is then baited with a plastic lizard or worm. The rig, which is dragged along the bottom of the deep water, is excellent for catching bass.

The smallmouth bass tend to stay along the rocky areas in the lake, which include Block Point, Coates Point, Hawkeye Point, Anthony's Nose, Friend's Point, and the many sunken islands in the North Basin. The numerous islands found in the narrows can also be excellent places to find smallmouths. In the southern end of the lake, islands such as Dome, Elizabeth, Long, Canoe, and Diamond are excellent choices.

Smallmouth bass will stay shallow until around July 1. They can be easily caught using chartreuse spinnerbaits, pumpkinseed-colored jigs with pork combos, and top-water bait such as the Pop-R or Sluggo. As the water warms, smallmouths move into deep water that ranges from 30–90 feet. These fish can be caught on jigging spoons such as a ½-ounce Hopkins Shorty, jigging just off the bottom. Carolina rigging may be another alternative.

In most lakes, the bass will move back to the shallows as fall arrives, but in Lake George, the bass stay deep and sometimes move even deeper. An example of this pattern was seen in September 1995 when Bass Anglers Sportsmen's Society (BASS) held its Eastern Divisional on Lake George. Most of the small-

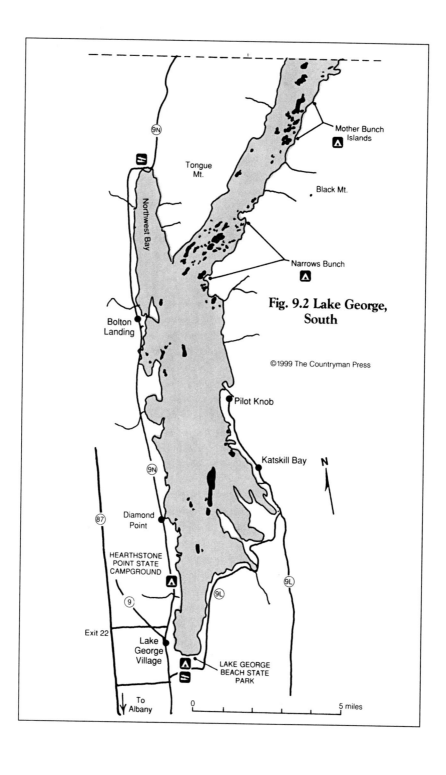

Fig. 9.2 Lake George, South

©1999 The Countryman Press

Mother Bunch Islands

Black Mt.

Tongue Mt.

Narrows Bunch

Northwest Bay

Bolton Landing

Pilot Knob

Katskill Bay

N

Diamond Point

HEARTHSTONE POINT STATE CAMPGROUND

Exit 22

Lake George Village

LAKE GEORGE BEACH STATE PARK

To Albany

0   5 miles

mouth were caught in 60–90 feet of water, and the largemouth were caught in 20–50 feet. There are several bass tournaments held on Lake George every year, among them the New York State Bass Chapter Federation, which has been holding its season opener there for the past 16 years. Lake George is considered to be one of the great bass lakes in the northeast. The average bass in Lake George weighs between 2–4 pounds, with lunkers caught in the 6-pound range.

OTHER COOL-WATER SPECIES

The northern pike and pickerel season begins the first Saturday in May and closes March 15. The best fishing is in the spring when the pike and pickerel are still in shallow water. They can be caught easily using lures (such as chartreuse or white spinnerbaits or Rapala-type plugs in a perch or smelt pattern) or live bait (such as shiners or sucker minnows). As the water warms, the fish tend to move deep, just like the bass. Covering a lot of water in the 30–40-foot range by trolling plugs or using live bait can be very productive. Good places to look for the pike and pickerel are the weed beds in the areas of Bolton Landing or Dunham Bay. Also, Northwest Bay and Harris Bay in the South Basin and Blair Bay in the North Basin are good bets. The lake has a good population of pike and pickerel, with the pike averaging 4–6 pounds and the pickerel averaging 3–5 pounds.

Panfishing in Lake George is productive-year round. Both crappies and yellow perch can be easily caught. In the spring, large crappies can be caught in shallow water off wooden docks along the shorelines in Bolton Landing, Huddle Bay, or Dunham Bay. Small white and chartreuse hair jigs, tube jigs, or small minnows on a bobber seem to be what attracts the crappies best. The rest of the year, the crappies can be found in 20–25 feet of water near wooden structures. The yellow perch in Lake George can be caught just about anywhere in the lake where grass is on the bottom and in 25–40 feet of water. Light blue line baited with small jigging spoons, small hair jigs, rubber jigs, or live bait has proven to be very productive when fishing for yellow perch. The average-sized perch weighs about 1 pound; a large one is in the 2-pound range.

TROUT AND SALMON

Lake George cold-water species, like the lake trout, can be caught year-round with no set season, but they must be at least 18 inches in length. There is a limit of three of each on lake trout and landlocked salmon. The trout and salmon feed primarily on smelt. In the spring when the smelt are spawning in the many creeks that empty into the lake, the trout and salmon can be found in the shallow waters feeding on these fish. Trolling the shorelines with planer boards rigged with trolling spoons, small Rapalas, or other stick baits seem to work well. Spoons such as Evil Eyes, Suttons, and Mooselook Wabblers and stick baits such as Rebels, Rapalas, and Bombers, all in smelt colors, work very well. Trolling streamer flies also works very well for salmon. As spring turns to summer and the water warms, the trout and salmon move deep, to 70–120 feet, making it necessary to use downriggers to even consider catching one of these fish. The best technique for fishing this deep consists of using a large 3- to 4-foot string of spoons referred to as a Christmas tree. On the end of this rig is usually a 3- to 4-foot leader with spoon or stick baits tied to the end. This rig is trolled right on the bottom. In the North basin, the trout and salmon can be found from Hague north to Friend's Point. Also, the areas known as Roger's Rock, Anthony's Nose, and Hulett's Landing to the Mother Bunch Islands seem to hold a good quantity of trout and salmon. In the South Basin, the trout and salmon can be found in the vicinity of Diamond Point, Tea Island, Long Island, Warner's Bay, and along the drop-off near Tongue Mountain Point.

DEC no longer stocks lake trout here, because they reproduce naturally and the population has stabilized at a desired level. However, landlocked salmon continue to be stocked each year and will be until optimal levels are achieved. These fish thrive on smelt, and the best fishing coincides with the smelt's spawning run, which begins shortly after ice-out (anywhere from late March to mid-April) and continues into May. Try trolling or drift-trolling off shore from smelt spawning streams, about 200 yards out with spoons like the Miller or Sutton Flutters or Lake Clear Wabblers with a trailing worm. Other proven lures are Mooselook Wabblers; Mooneyes in silver, gold, or copper;

crankbaits, such as Rapalas and Rebels in smelt colors; and J-Walkers. Early morning and late evening are the most productive hours. Fly-rodders will do well trolling Grey, Black, or Green Ghosts; Meredith Specials; Supervisors; Nine Threes; Dark Montreals; or any other smeltlike streamer that leaps from the vise screaming to be fished. You might even pick up a rainbow as a bonus. There's a small population that have drifted down from the numerous feeder streams. Interestingly, there is a growing cult of fly fishermen who take salmon in late April by wading out on the Million Dollar Beach in the village of Lake George. The fish are there looking for smelt on their way to spawn in West Brook, and it's as good an excuse as any to limber your casting arm after a long winter. If you're so inclined to get out and cast some streamers or nymphs in this early season, take the necessary precautions to avoid hypothermia—the water temperature will be well below 50 degrees.

Just after the smelt spawning run ends, the salmon and lake trout will gradually move to slightly deeper water as the warming temperatures force them down to between 35 and 90 feet, where they are usually found in early June. This is the time for downriggers or wire or lead core line. In the hottest months of July and August, the salmon may be down 50–90 feet, but you'll have to go even deeper for the lakers, which will have found comfort between 100 and 180 feet.

In the North Basin, the salmonids concentrate from Hague north to Friend's Point, from Roger's Rock to Indian Kettles, between Blair and Gull Bay, and from Hulett's Landing to Mother Bunch Islands off Roger's Rock.

In the South Basin, the lakers and landlocked salmon are found between Diamond Point and Tea Island, between Long Island and Warner's Bay, across the mouth of Dunham Bay, and along the drop-off near Tongue Mountain Point. Summer fishing for salmon and lake trout is a game of odds, and an electronic fish locator is now a necessity. Successful anglers know that salmon are comfortable in 50- to 60-degree water but feed in water 55–64 degrees. Lake trout seek comfort at 48–55 degrees and feed in a strata of 49–52 degrees.

In the fall, both species are fairly scattered as the water temperature is cooler and more uniform. Sweep-trolling down to 40 feet is the preferred method and offers a welcome return to light tackle as the fish, once again, are found closer to the surface.

The landlocked salmon of Lake George are famous for their skyrocketing jumps and drag-testing runs. An extra rod trolled with the lure in the propeller wash, about 15 feet behind the boat, can be an effective trick if the fish aren't taking. These fish will average 2–3 pounds, though many between 4 and 6 pounds are taken. Once you hook one, you'll swear they are bigger. The lakers run 8–12 pounds, but trophy fish of 15–18 pounds are landed each year. Anyone fishing Lake George should be aware that the use of smelt as bait (dead or alive) is prohibited. Also, any foul-hooked salmon or lake trout must be released.

ICE FISHING

For those seeking winter sport, ice fishing has always been popular on Lake George. The first freeze in the coves usually occurs in late November with safe ice generally found just before the new year. Tip-ups with minnows are standard for northerns, lakers, and salmon, but in late February, those big jack perch seem to come into their own. The game plan then changes to small minnows about 2 inches long and jigging spoons like the Swedish Pimple. Adding a perch eye always seems to increase the action.

Hot spots for lake trout and landlocked salmon include the Paulist's Fathers area in the South Basin, as well as the ice around Dome Island. Huddle Bay also provides its share of tripped flags.

For northerns, try Northwest, Warners, or Dunham Bay. Again, remember the importance of a steel leader.

The perch beds seem to change slightly from year to year, but Tea and Dome Island remain pretty consistent. Perch fishing through the ice is a social sport on Lake George, and finding the perch generally means finding the other ice fishermen—usually an easy task. Bring your best fishing and hunting stories (the true ones!), and be sure to dress for the cold.

CHARTERS

There are quite a few charter boats on Lake George captained by knowledgeable guides who advertise in local papers, through brochures at tackle shops, and—as often as not—through word of mouth. They are capable of furnishing all equipment and generally operate from inboard/outboards ranging from 20–26 feet. Combination packages are offered for both cool- and cold-water species.

Guides recommend trolling speeds of about 1½ miles per hour for deep fishing for lake trout and up to 5 miles per hour for landlocks near the surface. Trolling speeds vary with the species, depth, and lures. Advanced reservations are a must as these guides are usually quite busy with repeat customers.

If you bring your own boat, you should be aware that most bays and passages are zoned with a 5 mile per hour speed limit and that navigation lights must be used from sunset to sunrise. Also, the following buoy code will be helpful to ensure safe travel:

- Black and white spar buoy—Marks shallow water. Do not pass between buoy and shore.
- Red buoy with red flashing light—Standard channel marker rules.
- Green buoy with green flashing light—Standard channel marker rules.
- White with quick flashing white light—Shallow water nearby.
- Red pennant—Small craft warning of storm or high winds.

A WORD ABOUT MILFOIL

Some controversy, not to mention apprehension, has arisen as a result of a new weed problem in Lake George. The source of the issue is Eurasian milfoil, *Myriophyllum spicatum*. This extremely prolific aquatic plant poses a hazard to water skiers and gets a jaundiced look from camp owners and lake users who have had their swimming and docking areas invaded. Primarily a South Basin problem, the first growths of this weed were welcomed by bass and pike fishermen who found great fishing around the new weed beds. The increase in cover initially enhanced the habitat. Unfortunately, this weed multiplies at an astounding rate. Soon the weed beds became so impenetrably thick that they were all but impossible to fish except around their edges. Any perceived benefit of the plant here was thus short lived. Worse, milfoil's density encourages algae and scum growth, which adversely affects water quality and has ruined areas that were once used for spawning. Fortunately, the weed does very poorly at depths of more than 20 feet. The Lake George Association recommends hand-pulling for removal and has even gone so far as to cover areas of the lake bottom with a black plastic mat in order to block sunlight, thereby inhibiting growth. Time will tell what the long-range effects of this insidious plant will be, but solutions, if there are any, are not apt to be easy.

ABOUT THE AUTHOR

Robert Zajac is an active outdoorsman who focuses his attention on fly-fishing and big-game hunting. In the spring, he can be found chasing the hatches throughout New York State. June through August are reserved for Atlantic salmon, while in autumn he is out pursuing whitetails. He has contributed to several other books and has had articles published in the *Atlantic Salmon Journal*.

Keeseville's Ricky Doyle is the 1997 New York State Bass Anglers Sportsmen's Society (BASS) champion. He has competed in the BASS Regionals as a New York representative for the past 6 years.

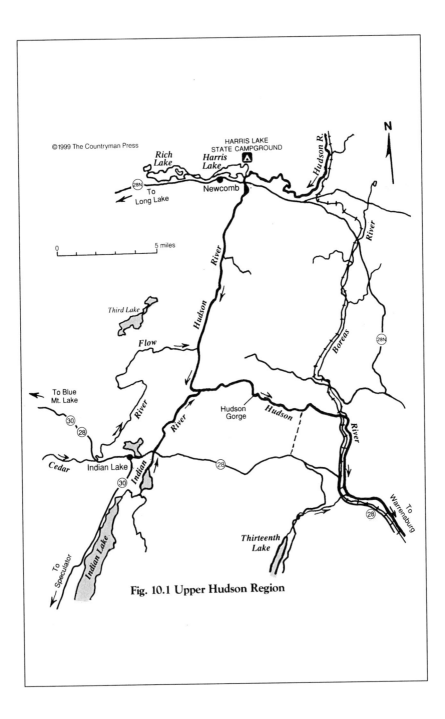

© 1999 The Countryman Press

Fig. 10.1 Upper Hudson Region

CHAPTER TEN

The Beautiful Tahawus Region

ROBERT ZAJAC

The civilization of the central Adirondacks began in 1826 with the chance meeting of an ambitious prospecting party and a controversial Abenaki Indian. David Henderson and Archibald MacIntyre hired Lewis Elijah Benedict to lead them to the iron ore deposits that had been the Native Americans' secret. They turned his fee of $1.50 and a tobacco plug into millions when they founded the Adirondack Iron Company a few years later. They called their guide Tahawus, the Indian name for Mount Marcy, meaning "he splits the clouds." Henderson and MacIntyre left their names on the mountains above Sanford Lake, and the settlement near the original forge still bears the name Tahawus.

The industry spawned towns, and roads linking them have evolved into paved highways. The Tahawus region is accessed by I-87 and Routes 28, 28N, and 30/8 and consists of portions of Essex, Hamilton, and Warren Counties.

Today, lodging, campsites, food, supplies, tackle, and bait are available in Indian Lake, Speculator, Wells, North Creek, and at most exits along the Northway (I-87). The Department of Environmental Conservation (DEC) office in Warrensburg offers a variety of printed material regarding stocking lists, guide services, and maps and is an extremely important source of information. Fishermen are urged to consult the regulations, which vary considerably by location.

WHEN TO FISH THE TAHAWUS REGION

Timing your fishing trip to this region is important. Winter is the prodigal son among Adirondack seasons. His tantrums can be felt through April, postponing the early spring enjoyed elsewhere. On many still waters, ice-out doesn't occur until late April, and the streams are not sufficiently warmed until May. From May through June is blackfly season, and an effective repellent is a wise investment in predator control.

Peak fishing for trout and salmon is generally from mid-May through mid-June. Because these species are extremely temperature sensitive, the best daytime fishing is before the heat and low-water conditions of summer. The fishing picks up again considerably in September. The fish seem to feed with urgency during the change of foliage, as if they sense the approach of the harsh winter.

WHERE TO GO

The Hudson River begins as a trickle from Lake Tear of the Clouds. Its flow increases as it is joined by the Opalescent, Indian, and Boreas Rivers. In the spring, it is a powerful river with magnum currents that demand respect when wading. From its junction with the Indian below Blue Ledges downstream to North River, the Hudson offers some of the area's finest fishing for brook, brown, and rainbow trout. A popular stretch of water lies adjacent to Route 28 in North River. For those willing to hike, the upper Hudson offers opportunities for a distraction-free escape to a primitive wilderness area. The spectacular Blue Ledges can be reached from the east side of the river by following the North Woods Club Road outside of Minerva to the DEC parking area at the Blue Ledges trailhead. Anglers willing to test their wading skills will be challenged by a variety of riffles, flats, pools, and pocket water. Waders with felt soles are recommended to ensure the best possible footing. Those who choose not to take this precaution are usually seen doing the Tahawus Shuffle. This sequence of gyrations and spastic gestures bears a marked resemblance to the Indian Rain Dance and generally results in a good soaking.

En route to the Blue Ledges, the hiker will cross the Boreas

River. This stream should not be overlooked as it offers good rainbow and brook trout fishing. It can be fished upstream or downstream from the crossing point and is a favorite among local anglers, especially near the still water about a mile upstream.

Below the town of North River, the Hudson is a series of long shallow flats with the occasional deep pool. As one proceeds south toward Glen Creek, the habitat becomes more conducive to smallmouth bass. They seem to occupy any pool offering reasonable depth.

Glen Creek enters the Hudson from the west and has some very large brown trout that tend to lose their natural caution during a good evening hatch. Although Glen Creek is stocked, the best fishing is near its entry with the Hudson and for a short distance upstream.

The Indian River is a productive trout fishery and can be reached by following Chain of Lakes Road north from Route 28 just east of Indian Lake village. The fishing begins just below the spillway and offers brook, brown, and rainbow trout for several miles to its junction with the Hudson. For those who wish to escape the crowds near the dam, the area above and below the Cedar River junction farther downstream is excellent and receives very little pressure. Caution is advised when fishing the Hudson and the Indian as their flow is regulated by the Hudson River/Black River Regulating District. Severe and sometimes sudden fluctuations in water level can occur.

The Sacandaga River and its East Branch are generally accessible as Routes 30 and 8 are rarely far from their banks. The main branch from Speculator to the town of Hope is fair trout water. Augur Falls below Speculator is a photographer's delight. Better fishing is found in the Wells area, just below the Lake Algonquin dam, behind the local lumber yard, and in the pools adjacent to the parking areas along Route 30 just south of town. The falls below the dam provides increased oxygen, and the series of pools downstream have sufficient depth to sustain trout through the summer. As the river flows south toward the Sacandaga Reservoir, it becomes more shallow, wider, and much warmer, creating habitat for smallmouth bass and panfish. The best of the East Branch is found by hiking north from the

A boat cuts through the early morning mist as an angler baits up a hook in the shadow of Tahawus.

Siamese Ponds Trailhead on Route 8 over Eleventh Mountain. In the cool valley below, one can enjoy solitude and brook trout.

Other streams worth a few casts are the Jessup and Miami Rivers north of Speculator and Mill and North Creeks in the township of Johnsburg, Warren County.

BE PREPARED

Although not as fertile as the Catskills, this region does have an insect population that generates considerable activity from May through September. Intercepting the hatches is an iffy situation anywhere, so fly fishermen should be prepared to try subsurface techniques, including streamer fishing and upstream nymphing. The Black-Nosed Dace, Mickey Finn, and Woolly Bugger streamers (4–8) and Gold-Ribbed Hare's Ear and stonefly nymphs (8–14) are consistent producers. During July and August, feeding activity is generally confined to early morning and late evening when the water is cool. Exceptions occur during cold, overcast periods when the rivers escape the heat of the sun. It is noteworthy that on occasion, rainbows can be "pounded up" by fishing pocket water with high-floating dry flies such as the popular Wulff patterns. These fish seem to prefer the faster currents and can be quite cooperative with this method.

Fly tackle for fishing the streams requires a rod of 7–8½ feet for a 5- or 6-weight line, enabling the angler to present a variety of fly sizes by varying leader length and tippet size. The length of rod is usually a personal choice, with the shorter rod favored for smaller streams.

The spin fisherman should be appropriately equipped with light tackle capable of handling 6-pound test and a variety of spinners and spoons in the ¼-ounce range. The Mepps Spinner, Mepps Minnow, Panther Martin, Phoebe, and Little Cleo are all very effective. A favorite bait-fishing technique is working a minnow or worm on a #6 hook below a split shot through the riffles and into the depths of the pools.

INDIAN LAKE

For those who prefer lake fishing, Indian Lake is highly recommended. Located in Hamilton County, this 4,500-acre impoundment offers beautiful scenery, easy access, and a variety of fish. Canoe and boat rentals are readily available, and there is a state boat launch. State campsites are located on shore and on several islands as well.

A season on Indian Lake begins in May with northern pike fishing. Techniques include trolling large spoons close to shore and still-fishing large minnows or suckers below a bobber in the shallows. The Lake Abanaki area adjacent to Indian Lake near Sabael is popular and produces northerns in the 4- to 10-pound range. There is also a smelt run in May where Squaw Brook enters Indian Lake on the west side.

Beginning in June and continuing through the summer, fishermen are busy casting for smallmouth bass in the 2- to 3-pound class. A jig-and-pig, various crankbaits, spinners, and spoons are all productive especially on the south and west sides of the lake's many islands. As with many constructed lakes, the bottom is composed of a variety of structure, which attracts gamefish. The rock ledges along the east shore are an indication of good water and deserve considerable attention. In the early morning and again later in the evening, top-water plugs such as the Hula Popper, Jitterbug, and floating Rapala provide exciting bass action, with northern pike adding an occasional explosive surprise.

The best area for landlocked salmon and lake trout is the north end of the Indian Lake just above the dam where the water covers the original streambed. Standard trolling techniques will take the occasional fish, but trout fishing has fallen off in recent years because of the severe fluctuations in water level that are due to dam releases in the spring and fall.

In addition, Indian Lake has an abundance of perch, bullheads, crappies, and other panfish available to the fisherman armed with worms and small children. It is an ideal spot for a family vacation.

THIRTEENTH LAKE AND OTHER PONDS

There is a special magic associated with brook trout fishing in an Adirondack pond. The horizon is always a distant mountain, and the quiet pace can be hypnotic until broken by a rising fish. Thirteenth Lake, Kibby, Peaked Mountain, Puffer, and the Siamese Ponds in Warren County are typical of the region. Hamilton County offers Tirrell, Owl, and others, such as Mason Lake with its added bonus of brown trout.

Spin fishermen generally cast bait, spinners, or small spoons while locals, a generation older, cling to the tradition of trolling a worm behind a Lake Clear Wabbler. These techniques are on the decline in recent years because of the DEC's efforts to protect these fragile ecosystems. In many ponds, anglers are prohibited from using live bait of any kind as the present population of trout is the product of countless dollars and hours of effort required to reclaim these fisheries. Shamefully, a number of other ponds have been lost to coarse fish inadvertently dumped from the minnow buckets of violators.

In the late 1870s, Henry Barton began mining garnet in the Gore Mountain area. Ore containing these ruby crystals was abundantly imbedded in the anorthosite crust of nearby mountains as well. The mountains overlooking Thirteenth Lake bear the scars of man's lust for a precious stone. The anglers canoeing Thirteenth Lake bear the passion for other jewels: brook trout, brown trout, and landlocked salmon.

Thirteenth Lake is a narrow ribbon of water 2 miles in length resting between Hour Pond Mountain and Balm of Gilead Mountain. It is accessible by car and can be reached via Thirteenth Lake Road, which meets Route 28 just west of North River. At the parking area you will note DEC posters defining current special regulations. Legal size and creel limits may vary from year to year, but Thirteenth Lake has been "artificials only" since the DEC reclaimed and stocked it in 1972.

Perhaps the most common method of fishing the lake is the slow troll from a canoe or small boat, which allows you to peacefully cover the water and enjoy the glorious mountain scenery. A small nymph (10–14) trailing about 60 feet behind is generally productive throughout the season, but anglers should also be aware of the existence of other opportunities. The aggressive landlocks and larger trout thrive on an abundance of forage fish. The fish seem to congregate where Peaked Mountain Brook enters the lake about ½ mile down on the west shore. A smelt streamer can be deadly both in this area and at the far (south) end of the lake where beaver have dammed Buck Meadow Flow. The warmer temperatures of spring stimulate insect activity that continues until the summer's heat becomes oppressive. Although trolling may remain a part of the game plan, it is now time to have a second rod ready in anticipation of dry-fly activity. Opportunities are numerous when the lake is calm as risers can be seen from a considerable distance, but even the slightest breeze will ruffle the surface, making the telltale rings difficult to distinguish even at close range. Midday opportunities occur but at the mercy of the breezes. Shortly after five o'clock, though, the winds often settle down for the evening. The trout and salmon now cruise just under the surface in groups, or pods, selectively dining on the insect du jour.

Fish rise to *Callibaetis,* a size 16 gray mayfly, but the importance of this hatch is generally overshadowed by the presence of caddis flies that are usually on the water at the same time in greater numbers. The small mothlike caddis flies are seen in several life stages: resting on the surface just after hatching, hovering above the water during their mating flights, and dipping to the surface depositing their eggs. The most common sizes are 16 and 18, and again, the fish seem to be more selective to size than specific dressings.

The Elk Hair, Henryville, and skittering caddis fly patterns are equally effective, but the most difficult aspects of fishing the surface are not fly patterns but approach and presentation. The most efficient method of approach during these "glassed out" surface conditions is to stop paddling a goodly distance away and quietly coast to the fish, or get into position and wait until their feeding direction brings them to you. These fish are easily spooked, and the complexity of the situation is compounded by the fact that, unlike stream fishing where the quarry maintains a position in a feeding lane, fish in still waters cruise the surface. The constant movement of these fish requires that the angler determine direction, anticipate where the next rise will occur, and have his fly waiting there as the fish approaches. Light tippets, long casts, small flies, perfect timing, and flawless presentation are the components of success on any Adirondack still water. Taking fish under these conditions provides a great challenge but even greater rewards.

In May, June, and again in September, the hatches can present more challenges or more frustrations as the lake changes its menu. The caddis fly and mayfly activity continues, but careful observation will yield that the fish may now be stuffing themselves with Diptera. These mosquito-like chironomids are preferred in their pupal state. Just before hatching, the pupa rest suspended in the surface film, invisible to the angler who may believe that the fish are rising for no apparent reason. A size 16–18 imitation of these delicate minutae will produce if the angler maintains his discipline. The degree of difficulty increases dramatically here—the tactics are the same for the caddis and mayfly hatches, except you cannot see the fly you are fishing. You strike when there is a rise where you believe your fly to be. This is postdoctoral fly-fishing and a supreme challenge. It requires perseverance, a bit of masochism, and a little Zen.

In early June, brown-bodied, grey-winged Hexagenia mayflies of Homeric proportions emerge at the south end of the lake. The hatch usually occurs during the noon-to-three period, allowing the angler to intercept it casually. These insects are a

Bob Zajac with a fine trout taken in the Tahawus Region. At least a half-dozen good trout streams converge in this upper Hudson area.

hook size 8 4XL and demand attention. They will occasionally flutter and fall clumsily back to the water, bringing slashing rises from both trout and salmon. This is the hatch that brings the big fish up, and a good hex hatch is a spectacle that raises the hair on the back of your neck and leaves memories indelibly etched in your mind.

Although wading is possible, more area can be covered from a canoe. Long casts with nymph imitations stripped back will bring fish, but the greatest sport is to be had with the dry fly. It is essential that presentations are gently placed ahead of cruising fish, allowed to rest, and twitched slightly if necessary to induce a rise. Again, these fish have shown selectivity to size more than pattern, and large Wulffs, hairwings, and spider types such as the Grey Fox Variant all have their day.

During the heat of July and August, the hatches subside considerably. Although there is generally a hatch just at dark, most fish are taken during the day by deep trolling.

Long rods are an asset for trolling but more important for dry-fly fishing from a boat or canoe. The additional length of an 8½- or 9-foot rod allows the seated angler to increase casting distance by simple laws of physics. Any good single-action fly reel with a light, smooth drag will do nicely. Line weight for trolling is not an issue, but trying to push a large fly during the hex hatch will require a 6- or 7-weight rod. For the more delicate presentations of smaller flies, an 8½-footer for a 5- or 6-weight line is about right. Leader length for dry-fly fishing the ponds should start at about 12 feet.

When playing landlocked salmon or any other leaping fish, it is imperative to "bow" to the fish when he jumps. This means, simply, that when the fish clears the water you should lower your rod tip to put slack in the line to prevent the fish from falling on a taut leader. The landlocks of Thirteenth Lake range from 10–21-plus inches, and 16 inches is a lovely fish. They are cousins of the majestic Atlantic salmon, king of gamefish, and as we bow to them we do so with respect for their genetic heritage.

Two-year-old brown and rainbow trout are now stocked here, and they average 12–16 inches on arrival. Holdovers are common.

The brook trout of Thirteenth Lake range from 10–18-plus inches, and a 14-inch fish would be considered a very good one. The beautiful brookie is the all-American boy that provides us with a link to a great era of Adirondack angling gone by and with a symbol of our obligation to preserve these fragile environs for the future.

ABOUT THE AUTHOR

Bob Zajac is a freelance writer who lives in Slingerlands, New York. He is a frequent contributor to the *Atlantic Salmon Journal* and spends much of the summer chasing salmon in Quebec rivers.

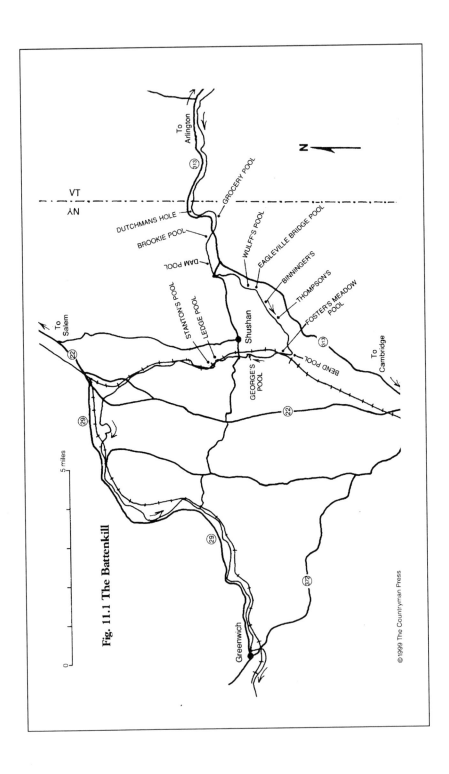

Fig. 11.1 The Battenkill

To Arlington

313

VT
NY

DUTCHMANS HOLE

GROCERY POOL

BROOKIE POOL

WULFF'S POOL

DAM POOL

EAGLEVILLE BRIDGE POOL

BINNINGER'S

STANTON'S POOL

THOMPSON'S

LEDGE POOL

FOSTER'S MEADOW POOL

Shushan

313

N

To Salem

22

GEORGE'S POOL

BEND POOL

To Cambridge

22

29

5 miles

29

372

Greenwich

0

CHAPTER ELEVEN

Washington and Saratoga Counties: Fishing the Eastern Slopes

TRACY LAMANEC, WITH WAYNE BREWER

This chapter discusses a beautiful region where lush farmland edges up against the foothills of the Adirondacks and Green Mountains. Washington and Saratoga Counties offer great fishing opportunities in their many streams, ponds and lakes. Many of these streams and ponds are privately owned, requiring anglers to seek permission from the owner. I will focus this chapter only on those waters that are open to the public.

WHERE TO FISH IN WASHINGTON COUNTY

The northernmost portion of Washington County is a narrow strip bounded on the west by Lake George and on the east by Lake Champlain. The New York–Vermont state boundary runs down the center of Lake Champlain. Here the southern part of the lake is very narrow, looking more like a slow-moving river than a lake. South Bay is the southernmost portion of Lake Champlain and is like a lake in itself.

This part of Lake Champlain offers excellent bullhead fishing in the spring. Big catfish are taken year-round, even through the ice, for those that know the secret of catching them. All kinds of panfish, especially yellow perch and crappie, are found here, too. Walleye and northern pike are abundant, as well as largemouth bass. I personally have found bass and an occasional northern pike on several types of structures: points, ledges, and channel edges; on the flats in and along the cattails; in and along the weed beds along the main lake channel and in the bays; and dragging a frog or other weedless lure over the top of weed choke areas or water chestnut. A friend tells me, "I enjoy taking my kids fishing from the bridge or state launch at South Bay because there is always something biting."

Ice fishermen find excellent crappie and perch numbers in South Bay and the other bays along the main lake channel. One ice angler recommends fishing smaller bays such as Mill Bay and Pine Lake Brook Bay. These are shallow and weedy, and have less fishing pressure, for great perch fishing. I have heard of pike up to 20 pounds taken through the ice.

Note: Remember, if fishing the Vermont side of the lake, you need a Vermont fishing license. These licenses expire on December 31.

The Hudson River separates Washington and Saratoga Counties from Stillwater to Hudson Falls. Most of this portion of the river has only recently opened up to catch-and-release fishing only, after being closed for approximately 20 years because of PCB contamination. Smallmouth and largemouth bass, pike, tiger muskie, and muskellunge are there for the catching. DEC stocked 52,000 muskellunge in the Hudson River in Washington County in 1998.

The Battenkill River is one of the best trout streams in the northeast. This storied river runs from Vermont to the Hudson River. From the Hudson, upstream 10 miles to near East Greenwich, the river supports a cool-water fishery. This would be a good stretch to use ultralight gear to have fun taking a lot of smaller smallmouth bass. After the first dam from the Hudson, tiger muskie are stocked (300 9-inch fish during 1998). Upstream from East Greenwich it is all trout waters. During 1998, 5,200 8½-inch brown trout were released in the Battenkill in the town of Greenwich. In the town of Salem, 9,120 8½-inch brown trout and 750 14-inch brown trout were released, and 3,600 8-inch brown trout were stocked from the air.

On the upper stretches of the Battenkill there are special regulations involving catch and release, and artificial lures only

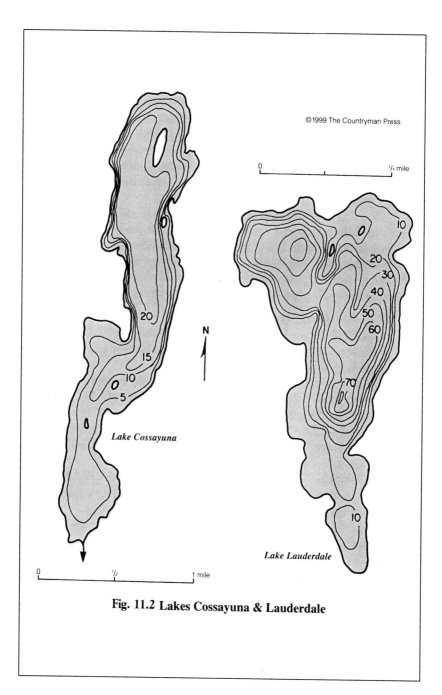

0   ¼ mile

10
20
30
40
50
60

70

20

15

10

5

0

N

Lake Cossayuna

10

Lake Lauderdale

0   ½   1 mile

Fig. 11.2 Lakes Cossayuna & Lauderdale

are allowed. Please refer to the *New York State Fishing Guide* for details about these restrictions. You should also be aware that other recreationists use this river to tube and canoe. If you are bound and determined to avoid them, fish early in the morning and late in the afternoon. Otherwise, let the tubers and canoeists pass when they approach you and continue to enjoy the fishing.

DEC stocked 450 8½-inch brown trout and 490 9-inch rainbow trout in the Poultney River in the town of Hampton in 1998. Minnow are recommended for early season fishing. One angler told me of good warm-water fish in the Poultney, including a great spring bullhead fishing.

The Mettawee River offers good rainbow and brown trout fishing. The pools and riffles harbor big rainbows. Salted minnows are recommended if fishing early in the spring. A total of 3,960 8½-inch brown trout, 500 14-inch brown trout and 4,330 8½-inch rainbow trout were stocked in the river during 1998. Here is a list of other waters stocked in Washington County:

- Indian River, Granville: 540 8½-inch brown trout stocked in 1998. You will find big rainbows in the pools and riffles. Again, salted minnows are recommended for early season fishing.
- Halfway Creek, town of Fort Ann: 2,070 8½-inch brown trout and 800 7-inch brown trout released in 1998. You'll find the larger trout in the big pools.
- Greenwich: 600 6½-inch brown trout released in Hartshorn Brook. The same was stocked in Mount Hope Brook in Fort Ann during 1998.
- White Creek, town of Salem: 1,460 8½-inch and 250 14-inch brown trout stocked. The Owl Kill (White Creek) also had 1,510 8½-inch brown trout released in it.
- Coy Brook, town of Hebron: 300 8½-inch brown trout stocked.

Wild trout exist in Camden Creek, Murray Hollow Brook, Steete Brook, Juniper Swamp Brook, and Black Creek. A bait fisherman who takes the time to talk to landowners and do some exploring can do well in these waters.

A string of ponds in the town of Jackson is worth seeking out: School House Lake, Hedges Lake, Clark Pond, Lake Lauderdale, and Dead Lake. These are all cold-water lakes, and access to the first three may be difficult because they are surrounded by private lands and camps. Dead Lake has access and is deeper and colder than the other lakes. Breeder trout are often released in this pond. In 1998, 1,700 8½-inch and 250 14-inch brown trout were stocked in this water. In Lake Lauderdale, 250 9-inch tiger muskie were released. Other stockings are as follows:

In the town of Dresden, Bumps Pond had 420 5-inch brown trout stocked by air, as were 530 in Greenland Pond, 740 in Lapland Pond, and 160 in Upper Black Mountain Pond. Clear Pond and Sawmill Pond both received 110 5-inch brown trout by air in 1998. Sprice Pond received 210 brown trout. Inman Pond in Fort Ann received 530 5-inch brown trout by air.

Cassayuna Lake (see Fig. 11.2) in Argyle has fine opportunities for northern pike, tiger muskie, largemouth bass, and panfish fishing. In 1998, 2,600 9-inch tiger muskie were stocked in this lake. Ice fishermen are also very successful on these waters. Smaller Lake Summit offers only shore fishing, but you might find yourself landing a big northern pike.

WHERE TO FISH IN SARATOGA COUNTY

Saratoga County has excellent fishing waters. On the east boundary is the Hudson River, which takes a turn at Hudson Falls and makes up a large portion of the northern border up to Lake Luzerne. As previously mentioned, that portion of the Hudson from Hudson Falls to the Troy Dam has been open only to catch-and-release fishing for the past few years. That portion of the river north of Hudson Falls has been open and offers good fishing opportunities. However, this portion of the river has not received a great deal of fishing pressure. Large northern pike and largemouth bass are common in that section of the Hudson above and below the Route 87 bridge. Likewise, yellow perch fishing is fairly good above the Route 87 crossing. In 1998, 61,000 ½-inch and 44,600 1-inch muskellunge were released in the Hudson River.

The rest of the northern border of the county from Lake Luzerne is carved out by the Sacandaga River, then Stewarts Bridge Reservoir and the Great Sacandaga Lake, which runs

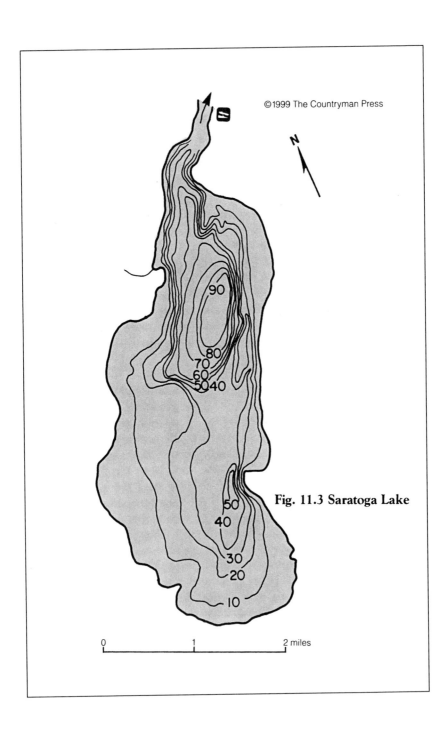

©1999 The Countryman Press

N

Fig. 11.3 Saratoga Lake

0   1   2 miles

down the western border to Fayville. The Great Sacandaga is known for its smallmouth bass, walleye, and northern pike and will be discussed in another chapter, but be sure to try the Stewarts Bridge Reservoir for walleye.

The southern border of Saratoga County runs along the Mohawk River from Waterford to Rexford. This portion of the Mohawk offers excellent smallmouth bass, tiger muskie, and northern pike fishing. Early in the spring, yellow perch and crappie are there for the taking. Fish those areas of heavy weeds and water chestnut and you'll find nice largemouth bass. Ice fishermen can find success fishing for yellow perch, crappie, and northern pike.

The best-known trout stream in Saratoga County is the Kayaderosseras. It is considerably smaller than the Battenkill and not as easy to fish. Most of its tributaries hold sizable brown trout, but few fly-fishermen are willing to try to cast in the confined quarters characterized by overhanging brush. A fat night crawler tumbled along the bottom following a summer thundershower is the best way to put one of those beauties in your creel. In 1998, 7,740 8-inch, 5,040 8½-inch, and 1,000 14-inch brown trout were stocked in the Kayaderosseras in the towns of Greenfield and Milton. In addition, 1,500 10-inch rainbow trout were also released.

To give you an idea of what other streams to fish in the county, lets look at the stocking records for 1998: Alplaus Kill in Charlton was stocked with 350 8½-inch rainbow trout. In the town of Northumberland, Snook Kill was stocked with 3,690 8-inch brown trout, and 540 8-inch brown trout were released in Cole Brook. Bog Meadow Brook in Saratoga and Geyser Brook in Saratoga Springs were each stocked with 300 8½-inch brown trout. Daley Brook (Corinth) was stocked with 590 eight inch brown trout. In Milton, 850 8½-inch brown trout were released in Glowegee Creek. LaRue Creek (Ballston) received 1,400 6-inch brown trout. In Edinburg, Paul Creek was stocked with 360 8½-inch brown trout, and Sand Creek had 770 8½-inch brown trout.

Ponds in that county were stocked as follows: Corinth Reservoir ponds got 400 8-inch brown trout. Upper Corinth Reservoir received 300 8-inch brown trout by air. Palmer Lake in the town of Edinburg was stocked with 500 4½-inch brown trout by air. Pettis Pond in Northumberland received 600 8-inch brown trout.

Moving on to larger bodies of water, Ballston Lake in Ballston has big largemouth bass and big pike, and larger than average crappie. Panfish, however, tend to be stunted. Also, there is good springtime bullhead fishing. A new fishing pier has been built at the north end of the lake and is open to the public. Access for larger boats than car-tops is limited to private launches. Ice fishing for perch and pike brings a number of anglers to the lake during the winter months.

Galway Lake in Galway is a fine cool-water lake, but access is limited due to private ownership. Round Lake and Little Round Lake in Malta offer fine largemouth, tiger muskie, and northern pike fishing. In 1998, 1,100 9-inch tiger muskie were released in these two lakes.

Saratoga Lake (see Fig. 11.3) is one of the best all-around lakes in the northeast region. Nice largemouth bass are in the weeds and lily pads, and smallmouth are in the gravel and rocky areas of the lake. Northern pike, walleye, yellow perch, and crappie are all abundant. My kids' favorite are those slab blue gills. In 1998, 8,678,800 ½-inch walleye were released in Saratoga Lake. We should not overlook Fish Creek at the north end of the lake; many pike and bass tournaments have been won out of Fish Creek.

Ice fishing is also good on the lake. But, be careful fishing around the mouth of the Kayaderosseras Creek and north down Fish Creek. There is current under that ice and it may not be safe. A good key is to watch where everyone else is fishing and fish there.

In the late spring and early summer, the large carp population in Saratoga Lake draws bow fishermen from all over the state. Bow fishing is a growing sport with specialized gear and boats. Twenty pound carp are common in the lake.

Smaller, but just as productive, is Lake Loney, connected to Saratoga Lake by the Kayaderosseras Creek. Contact the Lake Loney Marina for fishing updates on the lake.

Both Washington and Saratoga Counties offer great fishing opportunities. For the angler who takes the time to get permission from landowners to fish private waters and explore these waters, there are endless fishing opportunities.

Remember, before striking out for that stream, pond, or lake, check your *New York State Fishing Guide* for specific regulations on that body of water.

And please take a child fishing with you as often as you can!

ABOUT THE AUTHOR

Tracy Lamanec is a former member of the New York Outdoor Writers Association and an accomplished angler who knows the Battenkill River well.

Wayne Brewer, who uses the pen name Wayne Travis, is a freelance writer who lives in the Capital District. He has written newspaper articles on fishing Washington and Saratoga Counties, and he has fished pike and bass tournaments in many of the waters in the northeast. He is the author of *Enjoying Nature's Bounty: Recipes that Simplify Cooking Fish and Game,* a cookbook with over 300 recipes for big game, small game and game birds, waterfowl, fish, barbecue and marinades, seafood, wild plants and berries, and desserts.

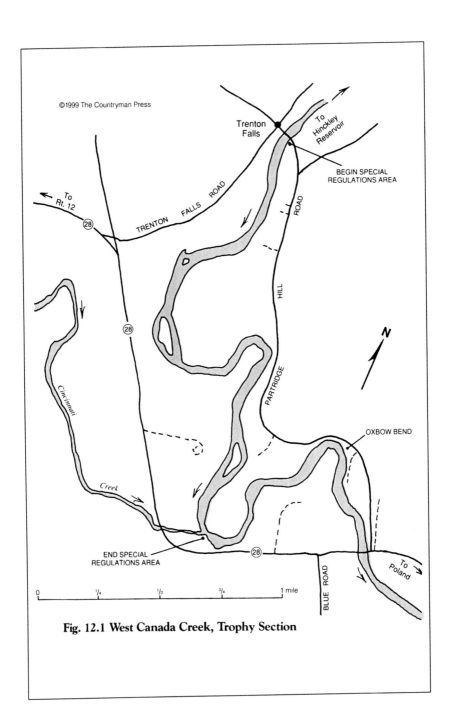

Trenton Falls

To Hinckley Reservoir

BEGIN SPECIAL REGULATIONS AREA

To Rt. 12

TRENTON FALLS ROAD

28

28

PARTRIDGE HILL ROAD

OXBOW BEND

Cincinnati

Creek

END SPECIAL REGULATIONS AREA

28

BLUE ROAD

To Poland

N

0   ¼   ½   ¾   1 mile

Fig. 12.1 West Canada Creek, Trophy Section

CHAPTER TWELVE

Exciting Fishing Just North of the Thruway

RON KOLODZIEJ

Wayfaring anglers using the New York State Thruway as a jumping-off point will find top-notch opportunities not only within the Adirondack Park Blue Line, but in the fringe areas as well. Let's consider one such area.

Spread out your map of New York State and locate Amsterdam, just west of Albany. Now draw a line due north to the community of Edinburg on the shores of Great Sacandaga Lake. From there extend your line due west to Alder Creek and then due south along Route 12 to Utica. Now trace a line over the Thruway back to where you started. If you fish anywhere within this roughly rectangular area, you're never much more than 35–40 miles from the Thruway, as the crow flies, but you have access to some 1,500 square miles of superb fishing opportunities, ranging from record-breaking northerns to bragging-size native brook trout.

GREAT SACANDAGA LAKE

Let's begin our odyssey at Great Sacandaga Lake on the eastern edge of our inscribed area. Created in 1930 as a flood control impoundment by construction of a large earthen dam at Conklingville on the Sacandaga River, this lake produced a world-record northern pike in 1940. It was a magnificent 51½-inch, 46-pound, 2-ounce fish that held the world record for almost 40 years. Although it was eventually bested by a European fish, it still lays claim to the North American record for that species.

The halcyon days for Sacandaga Reservoir, as it was then called, lasted through the mid-1950s. By that time the richly fertile farmlands inundated by the impoundment had leached the last of their nutrients into the water. Fluctuating water levels and a general lack of forage fish caused a gradual but perceptible decline in the fishery, but it eventually stabilized and still offers great year-round fishing for northerns, walleyes, yellow perch, and bass in-season. Conventional fishing methods for these species will work well on Great Sacandaga. Drift-fishing with Lake Clear Wabblers and a trailer hook baited with a night crawler or minnow is a good, productive technique for walleyes and perch. Cabela's Walleye Wobble Jigs in fluorescent red and green are proving to be excellent on the lake's walleyes. Drift-fished live bait can also prove deadly on that species. Sacandaga's smallmouths respond well to crawfish, hellgrammites, and minnows, but also to a variety of artificials, such as Mepps spinners and various crankbaits. The average Great Sacandaga walleye will weigh in the 1- to 2-pound range with 6- to 7-pounders being taken annually. Smallmouths will also average 1–2 pounds with occasional 5-pounders.

For the past dozen or so years, good-sized brown trout have become a welcome though infrequent bonus at Sacandaga for many anglers, including ice fishermen. Browns weighing up to 5 pounds have been reported, and though not present in great quantities, they do crop up often enough to have become less of a topic at local watering holes. These browns are products of stocking programs in area streams feeding the lake, and most are taken on live bait, though some fall prey to trolled spoons and spinners.

Over the years a number of big 8- to 12-pound catfish have also been taken in the lake, though the reader is cautioned against visiting Great Sacandaga specifically for that species. They're uncommon at best, and it's not known what their population level is or how they came to be in the lake. Escape from area farm ponds seems to be one plausible explanation.

Twenty pounds of Great Sacandaga northern. Fish twice this size may yet lurk in the lake where Peter Dubuc once took a world-record pike.

If Sacandaga's big northerns are your quarry, plan on shore fishing with big minnows. Few really big fish are taken by other methods such as casting or trolling. Trophy-hunting pike aficionados stake out a piece of accessible shoreline—generally in the lake's shallower southwest basin between the communities of Mayfield and Broadalbin—and rig up light saltwater or heavy-duty freshwater gear baited with 12- to 15-inch suckers. Then it's a waiting game. Prime time is May and early June when water levels are high and the northerns are still in the shallower, flooded portions of the shoreline before, during, and after spawning. If trolling is your preferred method, use large Daredevles in traditional red and white, or jointed Rapalas, Rebels, or similar lures in perch or other natural finishes. Depending on time of day, weather, water conditions, and depth, your best trolling speeds will be between 1½ and 2½ miles per hour. For the most part, you'll be trolling water less than 10 feet deep.

Boat launches are available at Northville on the Sacandaga River, at the Northampton Beach Campsite just south of Northville, in the town of Day in the northeast arm, and near the village of Broadalbin. These are state-operated, free facilities, but commercial launches can also be found liberally scattered around the lake. However, shorebound anglers on Great Sacandaga need not feel left out. Access to good shore-fishing areas is readily available along much of the lake's 125-mile shoreline. I recommend the areas around Northville and Batchellerville Bridges, along much of the Sacandaga River paralleled by Route 30, and numerous roadside areas in the lake's northeast arm.

STREAM FISHING AROUND GREAT SACANDAGA

Many of the streams draining into Great Sacandaga hold fine populations of brook, brown, and rainbow trout. You might consider Hans, Kenyetto, and Sand Creeks. These and other streams, including the Sacandaga River, are generously stocked with trout by the New York State Department of Environmental Conservation (DEC) and are generally lightly fished. Because of the nature of the terrain in the Great Sacandaga area, streams can range from slow-moving, sand-bottomed watercourses to typical boulder-strewn mountain streams with numerous pools and riffles. Any bait or tackle shop, service station, or general store can direct you to the nearest trout stream and can suggest the best way to fish it. Information available from the DEC and the Fulton and Saratoga County chambers of commerce will also help you pick out the streams you may want to fish.

PECK'S LAKE

We'll depart Great Sacandaga Lake region now and head west on Route 30A and 29A in search of other piscatorial adventures. A half-hour drive from Great Sacandaga brings us to Peck's Lake on Route 29A. This is an eminently fishable, privately owned body of water that holds excellent populations of northerns, largemouths, smallmouths, pickerel, and an abundance of panfish and has consistently produced prize-winning fish, including the second-place largemouth bass in the June 1989 edition of the big, statewide Genesee New York State fishing contest. It tipped the scales at 7 pounds, 4 ounces. This 1,400-acre lake has a maximum depth of about 40 feet and features the type of rocky, stump-filled structure that seems to spell fish. Launch facilities, camping, cottages, bait, and boat and motor rentals are available at the lake. Rates and additional information can be obtained by writing to the address at the end of this chapter.

THE CAROGA LAKES

A few miles north, near the intersection of Routes 10 and 29A, we encounter East and West Caroga Lakes, both top-notch fishing waters. They offer a mixed bag of everything from bass to splake to panfish. Walleyes have recently been stocked here and offer additional sport. The lakes are also popular ice-fishing destinations. The shorelines are pretty well filled by summer homes and camps, but fishing access is still available. There's a popular state-operated campsite on East Caroga, off Route 29A, and launch facilities are also offered. Boat passage between the two lakes is made easy by a small connecting channel.

CANADA LAKE

A stone's throw away, on route 10/29A, is Canada Lake. The 525-acre lake has a maximum depth of 144 feet and holds lake trout, which are stocked annually by DEC. Pickerel, small-mouths, and panfish are also present in generous numbers. There are commercial boat liveries on the lake as well as a state-operated launch site. Pine Lake, a few miles north of Canada Lake, also offers good pickerel, bass, and panfish angling.

NINE CORNER LAKE

Let's now do some walk-in fishing. Nine Corner Lake lies just west of Pine Lake and is easily reached by a gentle trail less than a mile long. The well-marked trailhead is located on Route 29A, a few hundred feet beyond where 29A and 10 part company. Nine Corner had suffered a bit from acid rain, but liming helped, and it receives generous annual infusions of brook trout. Shore-fishing access on this body of water is excellent, although a canoe or inflatable craft will help you cover more of the bays that give it its name. If conditions are right, you may even get a look at the resident loons. Fish this water as you would any north country pond, but I again recommend a Lake Clear Wabbler with a worm-baited trailer hook. It works as well on trout as it does on Great Sacandaga's walleyes. If fishing from shore, try small Mepps Spinners, Phoebes, and similar lures.

STREAM FISHING

We are now traveling west on Route 29A around Great Sacandaga. Various trailheads along the way lead the angler to other, more remote fishing waters. If stream fishing is your preference, you may want to consider any of a dozen or more streams that course through this area and harbor scrappy browns, brookies, or rain-bows. Those that are stocked annually by DEC include Caroga, Mayfield, McQueen, and Zimmerman Creeks, to name just a few. A good topographic or county map will help you locate these creeks as well as others that are not stocked but hold native pop-ulations of trout. DEC also publishes annual stocking reports, which can help you track down waters you may want to fish.

The next port of call in our westward trek along Route 29A and 29 is East Canada Creek. Flowing south out of the Ferris

Wild Forest, East Canada offers fine fishing for brookies and browns. It's a clear, cold-water stream that features deep holes, tempting riffles, and stretches that beckon to the fly fisherman. East Canada is good fishing water throughout the trout season, even during the warmer months. As we traverse Route 29A and then hook up with Route 29, bear in mind that the area to the north is as wildly beautiful and remote as areas found deeper in the Adirondacks. Fishing opportunities abound and are much too numerous to mention here, but this is where homework is important. Again, a good topographic map, some imagination, and all the information you can gather will open up dozens of new and exciting fishing opportunities for you.

HINCKLEY RESERVOIR
At Middleville, Route 29 hooks up with Route 28. Follow this road up to Route 365, and you're in the extreme northwest corner of our area. Here you'll find Hinckley Reservoir. With some 24 miles of shoreline, a picnic area, a boat launch, and a recreation area, it offers an excellent north country angling and camping opportunity. Hinckley is another of those mixed-bag waters with something for everyone—pickerel, some trout, bass, panfish, and more.

WEST CANADA CREEK
Let's backtrack now. That beautiful, tempting stream you were crossing and paralleling as you traveled northward on Route 28 was West Canada Creek, once rated in the top five of New York State's top 50 trout streams. To our Native Americans it was called Canata—stream of amber water. Primarily brown trout water, West Canada is popular and productive throughout the season, attracting trout fans of every ilk—waders, bank walkers, and canoeists. It supports a healthy native population of trout, generously complemented by some 30,000 hatchery-bred brethren stocked annually along its length. During the summer months it produces some good-sized bass in certain areas, but big trout are what you're here for. West Canada features big, deep, slow-moving stretches as well as faster water, offering every angler the opportunity to pursue his or her favorite method of angling. For most, however, this is prime fly-fishing

water, and all I can suggest by way of patterns is to "match the hatch." Mayfly, nymph, black gnat, Coachman—you name it, it will produce as on any other trout water at the appropriate time and place. Your favorite spinner or small crankbait will also work well. Bait fishermen will find that live minnows or worms drifted near the bottom will consistently produce trout.

In the early spring, West Canada runs high, fast, and cold, and this will dictate your fishing methods more than any other factor. The area below the dam at Trenton Falls is subject to sudden water releases from the power generating plant located there. There are no set schedules for these releases, and the wading angler should be constantly on the alert for signs of rapidly rising water. This is especially important in the trophy section below the falls, which begins at Trenton Falls Bridge and extends about 2½ miles downstream to the mouth of Cincinnati Creek. The creel limit is three, minimum size 12 inches, and artificial lures only are allowed. Route 28 parallels West Canada for much of its length, and roadside access is readily available for miles of excellent trout fishing.

Continuing south on Route 28, you can hook up with Route 29 at Middleville and head east through the southern reaches of our designated area. You're probably tired of fishing by now, but there's plenty left as we head back along Route 29 to Route 30 and our starting point. As you're heading back east along Route 29, plan on fishing Spruce Creek in the township of Salisbury. It's great water and harbors some fine brown trout. Spruce enters the East Canada at Dolgeville, and you'll be paralleling the creek for a while before entering the village. Other trout waters on your route back include Middle Sprite and Meco Creeks.

We've completed our cook's tour through waters inhabited by bass, northerns, trout, walleyes, bullhead, splake, pickerel, and every imaginable species of native New York State panfish—all a stone's throw from wilderness to the north and the Mohawk Valley immediately to our south. Staying on the roads plotted in this chapter will keep you within 25 miles of the New York State Thruway most of the time, but the angling opportunities you'll encounter are more than you could do justice to in a dozen seasons.

For more information, write the following local organizations:

- Fulton County Chamber of Commerce, 18 Cayadutta Street, Gloversville, NY 12078
- Great Sacandaga Lake Association, Box 900, Northville, NY 12134
- Great Sacandaga Lake Chamber of Commerce, PO Box 911, Northville, NY 12134
- Peck Lake Fishing Resort, Route 29A, Gloversville, NY 12078

ABOUT THE AUTHOR

Ron Kolodziej is an ardent fisherman and hunter who lives in Amsterdam, New York, and has fished extensively "just north of the Thruway." An outdoor columnist for the *Amsterdam Recorder* for more than 16 years, he has also written for *New York Game & Fish, Upland Fishing,* and southern Adirondack area newspapers. He is an active member of many outdoor groups, including the New York State Outdoor Writers Association, Whitetails Unlimited, and the Great Sacandaga Lake Fisheries Federation.

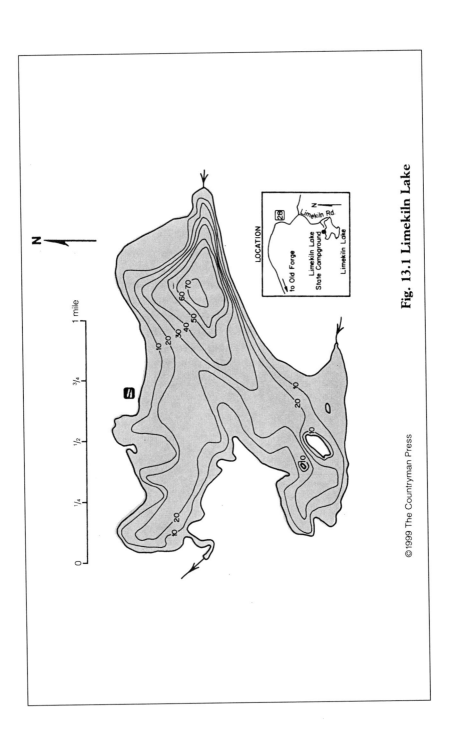

Fig. 13.1 Limekiln Lake

©1999 The Countryman Press

CHAPTER THIRTEEN

The Great Southwestern Wilderness

DON WILLIAMS

What is the most remote area in northern New York? This is a common question for both backpackers and anglers. Certainly, the Cold River area west of Mount Marcy is very remote. So is the interior portion of Tug Hill. And the upper Oswegatchie is very far from anything.

But perhaps the largest wild area of the Adirondacks is what we will call the great southwestern wilderness.

Nine topographic quadrangles define this region: Raquette Lake, Big Moose, Number Four, McKeever, Old Forge, West Canada Lakes, Piseco Lake, Ohio, and Remsen. This vast area encompasses some 1.3 million acres, much of it public or state land. Route 28 runs through the upper portion of this area, and Route 8 slices through the lower part. Both highways intersect with Route 30 (the Adirondack Trail) on the east and Route 12 on the west.

The southwestern Adirondacks abound with state land, some of it designated wilderness and some wild forest. Unit management plans have been developed by the Adirondack Park Agency and the Department of Environmental Conservation (DEC), and these define the usage of this part of the Adirondack Forest Preserve. The Ha-De-Ron-Dah Wilderness Area, West Canada Lake Wilderness, Moose River Plains Wild Forest, and Black River Wild Forest, along with portions of Pigeon Lake Wilderness, and Ferris Lake Wild Forest are all

165

found within the great southwestern tract. In this unspoiled setting you can hunt, hike, ski, canoe, and fish. In the wilderness areas, there will be neither sounds nor sights of civilization. In the wild forest areas, some motorized use may be permitted. Old wood roads and trails open up the remote fishing ponds and streams to the avid angler. State campgrounds include Alger Island, Brown Tract Pond, Fourth and Eighth Lakes, Golden Beach, Limekiln Lake, Hinckley Reservoir, Nicks Lake, Little Sand Point, Point Comfort, and Poplar Beach.

This region has spawned fish stories for a long time. In fact, stories of great catches have been circulating since the 1840 Lake Piseco Trout Club reports in the American edition of Izaak Walton's *Compleat Angler*. Those who read the book remember the 2 tons of trout taken from Piseco Lake in a 5-year period.

PISECO LAKE

Piseco Lake continues to bring good fishing to anglers today. It is especially noted for its good ice fishing. Lying close to Route 8 adjacent to Piseco village, it is easily reached over well-plowed winter roads by a drive through the village to the back side of the lake. About 2½ miles from the Route 8 turn to Piseco, you will spot the fishing shanties. In any event, stop before you get to the Poplar Point State Campground. The best fishing is off that point. Adirondack ice fishing can be very cold, but it can also be beautiful. A sunny winter afternoon on a snow-covered Adirondack lake, surrounded by mountain walls and good company, is truly an uplifting experience. Add to this image a 22-inch lake trout coming up through the ice, and the picture is complete.

Piseco Lake is stocked with lake trout yearly. One of the recent stocking lists included 8,700 6-inch lake trout. A winter catch may include a mixture of stocked and native trout. The natives are darker with some white at the edges of the pectoral and ventral fins. Stocked fish tend to have a more silvery color. Colors aside, lake trout is one of the most delectable of the trout family.

Anglers who find Piseco Lake to be one of the best winter fishing lakes around know how to get those lakers. They follow

The Great Southwestern Wilderness is for backpackers and boaters alike. Parts of this area are very remote and offer excellent trout-fishing opportunities in a wild setting.

the traditional ice-fishing methods: tip-ups baited with minnows securely fastened in the back with small treble hooks. The springing up of a tip-up triggers the angler's adrenalin, but a quick rush and a fast pull will lose the fish. The trick is to move slowly, let the hook set, and play the fish awhile. Caution pays off when a yellow-dotted laker is gently pulled through the open fish hole.

Piseco Lake is also a popular fishing lake during the warmer months. Good smallmouth bass fishing can be found in the north end of the lake. Stay near the middle and the west side; it is rocky near the island. Fishing off the weedy areas has also produced some bass for the summer fisherman. Whitefish, bullheads, perch, and pickerel are other species caught during the summer months. There are three state campsites on the lake—Poplar Point, Point Comfort, and Little Sand Point—with boat launching available at all three. Nearby hamlets can supply your needs, and the adjacent mountains, streams, and trails make it a great place to spend a fishing vacation.

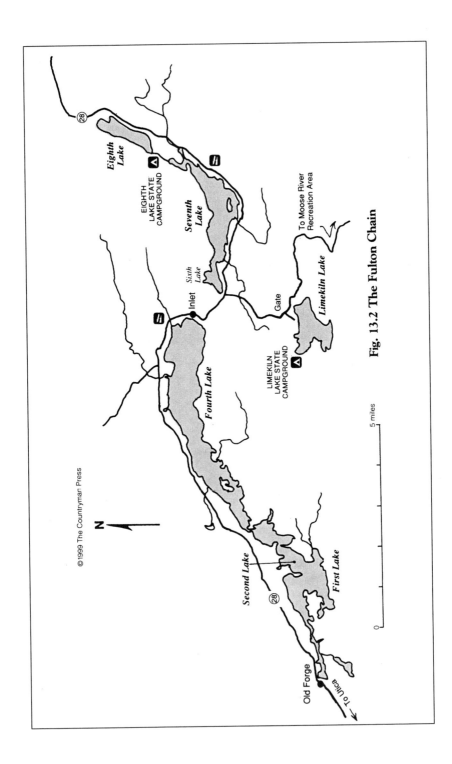

Fig. 13.2 The Fulton Chain

WEST CANADA CREEK

Another good fishing bet in the southwestern Adirondacks is West Canada Creek. Rising high in the Adirondacks, the creek is dammed by Hinckley Reservoir, then meanders down to the Mohawk River.

West Canada Creek was once listed in a New York State DEC publication as being near the top of the state's "Fishiest 50" trout streams. Good trout fishermen agree. It can be fished successfully from beginning to end. Much of the best fishing is found near the bridges, the old bridge abutments near Poland, fishermen's parking areas below Poland and above Middleville, and the roadside fishing areas between Newport and Middleville. The biggest fish are taken in the spring in the cold mountain waters above Hinckley. Good fish may be found near spring holes during the summer. The lower part of West Canada is discussed further in chapter 12.

The upper reaches of West Canada are remote and are right in the heart of the southwestern wilderness. State land surrounds the South Branch, which flows roughly east to west and joins the main river at Nobleboro. The main branch goes northeast up through the town of Morehouse to the West Canada lakes. Most of the main branch is surrounded by public lands. Fish the spots where feeder streams enter the main branch, and fish up into some of the feeder streams. The riffle sections are usually productive. Minnows and worms work best in the deep pools during the early spring; flies, spinners, spoons, small plugs, and worms work as the water warms. The most popular fly seems to be the Royal Coachman. Phoebes and Mepps are popular spinning lures.

LIMEKILN LAKE

Now move on to try your luck in Limekiln Lake. It can be reached by taking Route 28 east from Utica or Route 28 west from Blue Mountain Lake. Limekiln Lake is the western gateway for the Moose River Recreation Area. The entrance is reached by following a road running south and just east of the hamlet of Inlet.

Limekiln Lake is one of the cleanest bodies of water in the

state. It is rated "A"—safe to drink—although all water should be purified before drinking. The 460-acre lake also holds an "A" trout rating. The number of fish a lake supports is stated in pounds per surface acre, and at 100 pounds per surface acre we find that Limekiln Lake holds a good supply of fish. Limekiln Lake Campground offers a boat launch, so all of the fisherman's needs are present: a good lake, a supply of fish, nearby bait and tackle stores, a campground, and a launching site.

Splake have been stocked in Limekiln Lake for many years. Those who like brook trout and lake trout will love splake fishing, because a splake is a cross between the two. The state record is more than 11 pounds, taken from not-too-distant Eagle Lake 10 years ago. A 13-pounder was taken from the Adirondacks this past season but was not entered in the record books. It's just possible that a new record will be forthcoming. Regular catches range from 2–8 pounds. The cove areas of Limekiln supply some of the best summer fishing.

THE MOOSE RIVER PLAINS

Leaving Limekiln Lake we move into the Moose River Plains area, one of the wildest sections of the Adirondacks. Mostly state land, it abounds with fine fishing streams and ponds. The South Branch of the Moose River runs somewhat parallel to the southern side of the Moose River access road, and the road crosses several feeder streams. Other streams and ponds in the area can be reached via an extensive trail system. Secondary roads and old log roads also run through the area, providing additional access.

You may want to check the up-to-date regulations for the Moose River Recreation Area by getting the latest brochure from the DEC. No outboard motors are allowed, nor is the use of live bait fish. Other restrictions may also apply.

The Moose River was also listed in the "Fishiest 50." Besides the 30-mile-long South Branch of the Moose River, there is also the North Branch, which flows out of big Moose Lake near Eagle Bay, and the Middle Branch near Old Forge. Depending on where you fish, you may encounter brook, brown, or rainbow trout. All sections have brook trout, and the other species can be found from McKeever west. Once you are in the Moose River Plains, good fishing can be found almost anywhere. It is not unusual to catch a limit in the main stream or by fishing up one of the feeder streams. You may take any size trout during the season, with the daily limit being 10.

CEDAR RIVER FLOW

The Cedar River Flow is the place to go if you own a small craft such as a pram, guide boat, or canoe. It is a picturesque place to wile away your fishing hours, and it is well stocked with brook trout.

The Cedar River Flow is the eastern gateway to the Moose River Wilderness. It is best reached by driving to Indian Lake on Route 30 and continuing through the village, crossing the Cedar River bridge, and turning left at the next corner. You will see a cemetery on the left just before the turn. Proceed down the Cedar River Road until you reach the end. You will find the flow right at the entrance to the recreation area.

The Cedar River Flow is a great place to see trout feeding on flies and to try your luck at outsmarting them with some fly-casting. Worms also work, though according to Izaak Walton, "Our hands have long been washed from the dirty things, satisfied not to fish when the fly cannot be used"! If you don't subscribe to this, know that mountain trout also love grasshoppers and crickets. If all else fails, try a kernel of corn or a piece of tomato. They work!

The time of day is important in fishing these Adirondack waters. During the early spring and late fall, the trout feed during the middle of the day, especially when it is sunny. In the warm weather, trout are generally feeding during the morning and evening. In any case, watch closely for signs of surface-feeding, and you will multiply your chances for a successful catch. Fish the shores around the weeds when the Adirondack bugs are bouncing on the surface of the water.

For fishing such a large, remote area, you may want to give some thought to the hiring of a good fishing guide. Competent and reliable guides are available to make your trip safe and successful. Once the guide has shown you the fishing secrets in the

Cedar River Flow, the West Canada Wilderness, or the Moose River Plains, you can choose to go with or without a guide on your future trips.

THE FULTON CHAIN OF LAKES

The Fulton Chain of Lakes on Route 28 has long been popular for fishing. First Lake can be found sprawling east from the village of Old Forge, 50 miles northeast of Utica. The eight lakes stretch northeast for some 15 miles from that point almost to Raquette Lake. They can be seen and are easily reached from main highways. First, Second, and Third Lakes are closely connected by small passages. A longer, winding passage leads to the largest lake on the Fulton Chain, Fourth Lake. The hamlet of Inlet is at the head of Fourth Lake. Fifth Lake is a small pond not connected by passable waters to Sixth Lake. Seventh and Eighth Lakes are sizable lakes and along with Fourth Lake are popular fishing spots.

Fourth Lake is a good choice for a variety of fishing opportunities. Lake trout are taken in the spring along the shores, and from the middle of June through the summer they are taken from the deeper waters. The deeper areas out from Eagle Bay and south of Cedar Island are good spots for trolling. Start the season with silver Rapalas, and use some of your better "action" spoons later on.

Landlocked salmon, an introduced species, can be taken during the same periods. In the early season they are in the shallower areas, especially where the feeder streams come in. Minnow-imitating lures and flies are used. Trolling throughout the summer pays off. Try trolling near the surface during the early morning in the roughly triangular area formed by Cedar Island, Dollar Island, and Inlet. A New York State boat launch is located at Inlet right on Route 28. A marina and boat launch can also be found in Inlet, and a state launch site/picnic area is available at the end of Fourth Lake on South Shore Road.

Those who like shore-fishing will find Fourth Lake a good bet during May. A big attraction is the rainbows, which can be taken by casting from shore with live bait. A section near Route 28 just east of Barton Island holds good promise. Shore-fishing can be practiced throughout the summer, although trolling is the preferred method then. Add some "Christmas Trees" to your usual lures to attract the rainbows. The best spots are always near the islands.

Smallmouth bass are also present in Fourth Lake, with the best concentrations usually found at the east end of the lake and in the small bays along the south shore. Evening fishing pays off when pursuing the smallmouths here. Popular lures such as Hula Poppers, Rapalas, and Mepps are put to work, and crabs (crawfish) and minnows are employed throughout the season.

Brown and brook trout are found at the west end of Fourth Lake near Alger Island. Spin-casting with lures, fishing with live bait, and trolling with small plugs and spoons can all help to put a few browns and brookies in the frying pan.

Seventh Lake also has a convenient boat launch site on Route 28. The lake and the launch site are well marked and easily located. Seventh Lake provides much the same fishing as Fourth Lake, but it is not as large. New York State stocks Seventh Lake with rainbows, lakers, splake, and landlocked salmon. It is one of the best waters for splake fishing. Sixth Lake is also stocked with brook trout.

Eighth Lake is as popular as Fourth Lake in the Fulton Chain. The Eighth Lake campsite, 5 miles west of Raquette Lake village, provides access and a place to stay. Eighth Lake is stocked with rainbows, lakers, and landlocked salmon. Anglers come from miles around to get those rainbows during the summer months. Getting an early start pays off, and the best fishing spot is near the island in the east end. Trolling the section toward the highway with a Christmas Tree rig often attracts the rainbows that call Eighth Lake home.

REMOTE PONDS

One of the greatest outdoor experiences is to backpack and bushwhack into a remote pond for fishing. It is worth the effort, whether you choose to rely on your own outdoor skills or play it safe with a guide. Backpack angling moves fishing one step further from the norm and provides a challenge for those with the gumption to try it.

There are 174 ponds in the southwestern Adirondack area, and 88 of them hold a trout (T) designation. Study a topographic map and pick the one that looks best to you. The list includes three Beaver Ponds, six Buck Ponds, three Deer Ponds, four East Ponds, three Grass Ponds, six Mud Ponds, three Rock Ponds, and three Round Ponds—all rated for fish survival and/or trout. Some of the stocked ponds that you may see on the maps are Bear Pond, Bullhead Pond, Clear Pond, and Twin Pond. The complete list is available from DEC each year. Just pick a pond and make your plans.

PLANNING A TRIP

How do we do it? We select the area we want to fish from a topographic map. For illustration, let's pick the Old Forge Quadrangle. This quadrangle is number G210 on the key to New York State topographic maps. This number is important, in case the pond we pick is one of those several mentioned that share the same name. Fishing in the wrong pond could be an unsuccessful venture.

We may want to vacation and fish near the Fulton Chain of Lakes and also have access to the South Branch of the Moose River. We will make our base camp near Old Forge and locate a pond in that area for our fishing hike.

Bisby Road runs south out of Old Forge village to the Bisby Chain of Lakes (another fishing possibility). Almost 3 miles out of the village, the road crosses a trail that leads to Rock Pond at about the same spot it crosses the outlet of Little Moose Lake. Rock Pond is one of five waters by that name in the southwest Adirondacks. However, the one in this quadrangle is rated high for trout fishing.

The hike in to Rock Pond would take less than an hour, and for those interested, another short hike would take them to some fishing on the South Branch of the Moose River. Those motivated for an extended backpacking trip could spend several days in this area trying out the fishing waters.

Other ponds can be found the same way. Another example might be a look at a reclaimed trout pond such as Jakes Pond in the Number Four quadrangle. Some ponds are more remote than these, but the fish are there for those who want to go after them. No one can guarantee a successful trip, but your chances are multiplied when you get into the less-fished waters of the southwest Adirondacks.

ABOUT THE AUTHOR

Don Williams is an Adirondack guide, a retired school administrator and teacher, and former host of the TV program *Inside the Blueline*. Born and raised in the Adirondacks, he grew up at the trailhead to the Northville–Lake Placid Trail. He served 20 years as Adirondack regional editor for *New York Sportsman Magazine* and has contributed articles to *Adirondack Life* and other publications. He writes a weekly Adirondack newspaper column, "Inside the Blueline," for four newspapers and does historical reenactments of the Old Guide, Abraham Lincoln, Johnny Appleseed, and others. He resides in Gloversville with his wife, Beverly. They have five grown children and eleven grandchildren.

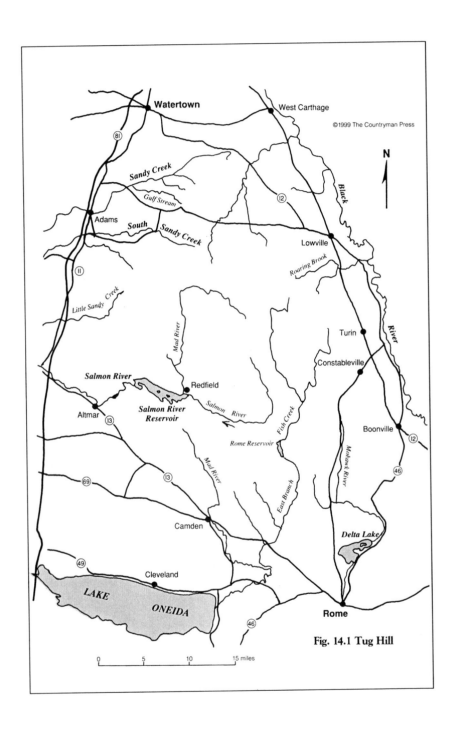

©1999 The Countryman Press

N

Watertown

West Carthage

Sandy Creek

Gulf Stream

Adams

South Sandy Creek

Lowville

Black

River

Roaring Brook

Little Sandy Creek

Mad River

Turin

Constableville

Salmon River

Redfield

Salmon River Reservoir

Salmon River

Altmar

Rome Reservoir

Fish Creek

Boonville

Mohawk River

Mad River

East Branch

Camden

Delta Lake

Cleveland

LAKE

ONEIDA

Rome

Fig. 14.1 Tug Hill

0   5   10   15 miles

CHAPTER FOURTEEN

The Secret Streams of Tug Hill

ALLEN BENAS

Tug Hill is a large, elevated land mass located in the northern New York State counties of Lewis, Jefferson, Oneida, and Oswego. While largely ignored by outside anglers, its 1,285,000 acres offer some of the best wilderness trout fishing opportunities in the state.

Although Tug Hill is little more than an hour's drive from Utica, Syracuse, and Watertown, it is time spent traveling back in history—back to the days when people were few, and the quiet remoteness of the surroundings made you wonder if anyone had ever stepped foot exactly where you were standing at the moment. This vast area, its silence interrupted only by the sounds of nature, is inspiring.

Today, Tug Hill is best known for receiving the greatest amount of snowfall east of the Rockies. Its average annual snowfall of 260 inches (with a record of 355 inches—that's 29.6 feet!—in 1971) makes it a major source of water for the Black and Mohawk–Hudson River systems. Recreationally, this snowfall makes the Hill one of the most popular cross-country skiing and snowmobiling areas in northern New York.

The area experienced its greatest population growth during the mid- to late 1800s. Because it was a prime timber area, towns grew, new timber camps sprang up, and the railroad expanded its service area to haul the tons of spruce, hemlock, and pines

177

needed by the growing cities that surrounded it. The timber industry prospered until the early 1900s.

Agriculture followed the timber industry. However, farmers faced with the combination of short growing seasons and extreme amounts of precipitation found their efforts exhausting and often futile. The majority of farms were deserted by the 1940s, and the land quickly reverted to a wilderness character. The demands put forth by nature created a bond among those who stayed on the Hill, as it did their fellow frontiersmen who had moved west decades before. Those who live on the Hill today have retained this feeling of togetherness and seem eager to extend their hands in friendship to those desirous of making the Hill a part of their lives.

FISHING IN TUG HILL

Tug Hill trout streams reflect the region and range—from small wild brook trout streams to larger streams (such as the East and West Branches of Fish Creek, which support populations of wild and stocked brown trout as well as wild brook trout) to the lower Salmon River (with large runs of steelhead, chinook, and coho salmon). With this diversity of angling opportunity, coupled with an array of streams too numerous to list, Tug Hill offers the trout hunter some fine fishing in a remote, uncrowded setting.

The headwaters of the Deer River, along with North and South Sandy Creeks, are located on the northern portion of Tug Hill in Jefferson and Lewis Counties. These streams are well known to local anglers for their excellent wild brook trout fishing, particularly during May and early June. The majority of fish are in the 7- to 10-inch range, but brookies up to 15 inches are not uncommon. The best baits are worms or small spinners. Spinners are most effective when cast upstream and retrieved downstream slightly faster than the current. Some of the best streams are Raystone, Abijah, and the upper reaches of South Sandy Creek in the vicinity of Worth Center. South of the hamlet of Barnes Corners are the East and West Branches of the Deer River, the upper reaches of the Mad River, Edick Creek, and Sears Pond. Also, North Sandy Creek above the village of

Winter dies hard on Tug Hill. Often, deep snowbanks will greet you on April excursions to the rich trout waters of the Hill.

Adams is stocked with brown trout, and each spring holdover trout in the 15- to 17-inch range are caught. These streams are generally small and brushy and best fished with short fishing rods and hip boots. Because the best fishing coincides with the peak of the blackfly season, a good supply of insect repellent is recommended.

The Salmon River watershed is located on the western slope of Tug Hill, primarily in Lewis and Oswego Counties. It flows westerly through Pulaski and enters Lake Ontario at Port Ontario. Above Redfield Reservoir, the East Branch of the Salmon is a high-quality wild brown and brook trout stream. The brook trout generally range up to 12 inches and are abundant. Brown trout are found in the deeper pools, and Department of Environmental Conservation (DEC) electrofishing surveys indicate that fish in the 15- to 20-inch range are common. However, the browns are difficult to catch, and best success is achieved by fishing early mornings or late evenings with large streamers or live bait.

These upper reaches of the Salmon River range from 20–50 feet wide, with pools in excess of 4 feet deep and a bottom of clean gravel. The water is gin clear, and a careful approach improves fishing success. Summer dry-fly fishing can be outstanding at times.

The state has acquired more than 20 miles of public fishing rights on the upper Salmon and its tributaries. Tributaries with public fishing rights that provide wild brook trout fishing are the lower Mad River, North Branch Salmon River, and Fall, Mallory, Stony, and Prince Brooks. These streams are similar to those found on the north slope of Tug Hill, and the same fishing techniques will prove effective.

Below Redfield Reservoir, the Salmon River supports the largest salmon and steelhead runs in the Lake Ontario drainage basin, providing year-round angling opportunities. Salmon in the 30-pound-plus range and steelhead more than 10 pounds are common. Effective techniques and angling locations vary with the seasons and timing of the runs. Current information can be obtained by calling the Oswego County Fishing Hotline (315-342-5873) or by contacting one of the numerous tackle shops in Pulaski. DEC's Salmon River fish hatchery is located on the river at Altmar and is open to the public daily. The hatchery raises steelhead, chinook, and coho salmon. *Good Fishing in Lake Ontario & Tributaries,* in this same series of books, covers the Salmon River in detail.

Between Lowville and Boonville in Lewis County, a number of streams flow down the east slope of the Hill into the Black River. The character of these streams is markedly different from those just discussed. They have steeper gradients, small waterfalls and gorges, bedrock and broken rubble streambeds, and more variable seasonal flows. Their upper reaches provide fishing for wild brook trout, while the lower portions are generally stocked with brook and brown trout. Wild browns are also present in a number of streams. Good fishing can be found throughout the season in Roaring Brook, Whetstone Creek, Douglas Creek, Mill Creek (Turin), House Creek, the Sugar River and tributaries, and Mill Creek (Boonville).

These streams have generally good access and can be fished effectively with spinning and fly tackle. Fishing pressure is low, and it is not unusual to catch trout in the 12- to 15-inch range. Whetstone Marsh Pond near the village of Martinsburg is stocked with tiger muskellunge and provides the unique opportunity to catch this hybrid of the muskellunge and northern pike. Tigers to 12 pounds are not uncommon here.

FISH CREEK

Undoubtedly the best trout fishing on Tug Hill is found on its south slope in the East and West Branches of Fish Creek, located in southern Lewis and northern Oneida Counties. The Fish Creek watershed is large, and both branches have numerous large and small tributaries. There are many road crossings. DEC has acquired approximately 55 miles of public fishing rights on the East Branch and its tributaries and 28 miles on the West Branch system. In spite of the high fishing quality and excellent fisherman access, fishing pressure is generally light.

The Oneida County section of the East Branch from the village of Taberg upstream to Rome Reservoir is big water with fast runs and deep pools. Along with a wild brown and brook trout population, portions of the stream are stocked with yearling brown trout. The East Branch provides excellent fly-fishing water. Large stonefly nymphs fished in the deeper runs in the early morning are particularly effective. Dry-fly fishing is also good, and there is usually a good green drake hatch in early June. This section is open to fishing until November 1, and spectacular catches can be made with minnows during late October, especially just below Rome Reservoir. Rome Reservoir itself is stocked with brown trout, and fish up to 4 pounds are fairly common. Fishing is difficult because of the large minnow population in the reservoir.

Fishing pressure in the Lewis County section of the East Branch above Rome Reservoir is light, although fishing quality is excellent. The stream provides good fly-, spin-, and bait-fishing opportunities. A favorite section locally is off the Stinebricker Road in the town of Lewis. The East Branch has many excellent tributaries. Generally, all the smaller ones support populations of wild brook or brown trout. Some of the larger tributaries that provide good fishing are Furnace, Florence, Fall, Point Rock, and Alder Creeks. Besides wild trout, the lower reaches of each are stocked annually.

In contrast to the East Branch, the West Branch is generally a slow meandering stream, particularly above the village of Camden in Oneida County. It is floatable from the Westdale Dam in Oswego County downstream to Camden. The section is hard to fish but can provide the determined angler with browns in the 2- to 4-pound range. Live-bait fishing is the most productive technique. Below Camden, the stream is similar to the East Branch, providing good fly- and spin-fishing for brown trout. Particularly good fishing can be found in the following tributaries: Little River, Mad River, Thompson Creek, and Walker Brook.

At the confluence of the two branches at Blossvale, Fish Creek begins the transition from a cold- to cool-water stream. Smallmouth bass and walleye become more frequent, but large brown trout in the 4- to 6-pound range are regularly taken on live bait. A particularly productive area is off Passer Road in the town of Verona.

Three other overlooked streams originate on the south slope of the Hill. They are the East and West Branches of the Mohawk River and the Lansingkill in the towns of Boonville,

Ava, and Western in Oneida County. All three provide excellent fishing for wild and stocked brown and brook trout. The Lansingkill in the gorge between Boonville and Westernville is particularly good. Both branches of the Mohawk have relatively long, tough-to-reach sections that provide excellent fly-fishing for brown trout in the 10- to 14-inch range for those willing to walk.

PLANNING YOUR TRIP

By now it should be apparent that county highway maps or appropriate United States Geological Survey (USGS) quadrangle maps are essential to finding the various streams and locations discussed. Highway maps can be purchased from the appropriate county clerk's office for a nominal fee. A key to the quadrangle maps for New York (to figure out which maps you need) can be obtained by writing to Distribution Branch, United States Geological Survey, Box 25286, Federal Center, Denver, Colorado 80225 (303-236-7477). USGS maps can be ordered from this address or through many book and sporting goods stores. If you're in a hurry for USGS maps, you can order them with a credit card from Timely Discount Topos (1-800-821-7609), which for a modest surcharge will send them out quickly. Contour maps similar to (but with less color than) the USGS quads are published by the state and are available from Map Information Unit, New York State Department of Transportation, State Campus, Bldg. 4, Room 105, Albany, NY 12232 (518-457-3555).

The ambience of the Hill is not a state of mind but very real. It offers an opportunity to relive what many consider the golden days of decades past . . . days when it was people against the elements throughout the year, and survival during the harsh winters was a daily chore. In truth, the type of experience that some anglers travel the world in search of can be enjoyed right here in this region of New York.

More in-depth information on Tug Hill is available from the Temporary State Commission on Tug Hill and the New York State Department of Environmental Conservation, both at the NYS Office Building, 317 Washington Street, Watertown, NY 13601.

ABOUT THE AUTHOR

Allen Benas is a widely experienced St. Lawrence River fishing guide and resort owner. He writes actively about the outdoors and is a member of the Outdoor Writers Association of America. Besides the St. Lawrence, he has fished and hunted farther afield, with the trout streams of Tug Hill being one of the places he dotes on.

CHAPTER FIFTEEN

Back in Time on the Oswegatchie

PETER O'SHEA

O ne of the most cherished adventures of early 20th-century sportsmen—a canoe trek up the legendary Oswegatchie Inlet of Cranberry Lake in pursuit of its fabled brook trout—can still be experienced by modern anglers. The truly large brookies that once tempted the nation's fishermen and famed naturalists like Ernest Thompson Seton for the most part no longer exist. Much remains, though, not the least of which is the wilderness aura, one that increases as the distance from the launching site lengthens. Amid the beautiful surroundings, one can still thrill to the pursuit of the smaller trout that are present today, both in the Oswegatchie itself and in Cranberry Lake, the body of water it feeds.

CRANBERRY LAKE

Cranberry Lake itself, now approximately 11 square miles in extent, doubled in size with the erection of a dam more than a century ago. The dam flooded not only part of the Oswegatchie but also many of the lake's small feeder streams. These flooded inlets, or flows, were once the place to fish for the lunker trout. The flooding also created a rather circular main body of water open to the west winds and a series of shallow, sheltered inlets spiraling away like the spokes of a wheel.

The inadvertent introduction of yellow perch around 1945

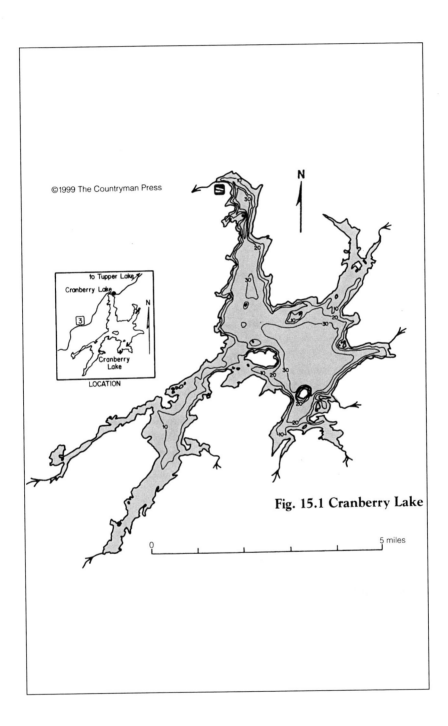

Fig. 15.1 Cranberry Lake

led to the rapid demise of the renowned brook trout fishery. Smallmouth bass were introduced about 1960, and a fairly successful fishery for this species was established shortly thereafter. However, in the late 1970s, acid rain begin to lower the pH of the lake, and this led to a sharp reduction in the number of yellow perch. With the decline of this competing species, brook trout became reestablished in Cranberry Lake starting about 1980. The lake is now stocked regularly with brook trout and, in addition, there is some natural reproduction over the gravel beds of the river inlet in autumn. There still remains some fair fishing for smallmouth bass on occasion. Deep casting in the flows can be effective, especially in late July or August. Fishing the deeper waters off some of the lake's many islands can also prove rewarding at this time. Sears Island is one that comes to mind; try using live crayfish here.

Early in the year and during September, carefully fishing the shoals off the various flows will prove most productive. These shoal areas are marked by buoys in some cases.

Both Rapalas of different colors and live minnows have proven effective on smallmouth bass through the years on Cranberry. Rock bass weighing as much as ½ pound are also present here, particularly in the flows. They are susceptible to worms and various small spinners. Dead Creek Flow is a good bet for both rock bass and the occasional lunker smallmouth bass. Smallmouth weighing as much as 6 pounds have been taken. Brook trout fishing in the main lake is often best in the flows, particularly just after ice-out in early spring. The Cucumber Hole, one of the many bays of Dead Creek Flow, often proves rewarding for brook trout fanciers at this time.

Cranberry Lake is reached by proceeding west on Route 3 for 26 miles from the village of Tupper Lake to the hamlet of Cranberry Lake. Both food and lodging are available in the hamlet. A Department of Environmental Conservation (DEC) campground is located just outside the village; turn south off Route 3 onto Lone Pine Road and go about 1⅓ miles to reach the entrance. It is usually open from Memorial Day through October. A bait and tackle shop is also located in the village.

Approximately 80 percent of the shoreline of Cranberry Lake is forest preserve, as are a number of the many islands that dot the lake, including Joe Indian (the largest). Designated sites have been assigned for primitive camping here by DEC. Boats may be launched from the DEC boat launching site located in the village on Columbian Road just south of Route 3.

THE FAMOUS OSWEGATCHIE

The main feeder of Cranberry Lake is the Oswegatchie River. It flows approximately 26 miles through the boreal woodlands of the forest preserve, from its source springs in a remote area south of High Falls to its mergence with the lake 2 miles below the hamlet of Wanakena. Except for a few short rapids in low water and one carry around a waterfall, the river is canoeable for 22 miles upstream from a public boat launching site at a noninhabited place on the river called Inlet (see Fig. 15.2).

Inlet, once the site of a sportsmen's hotel, is reached by turning south on a gravel road approximately 1 mile east of the village of Star Lake and heading south 3 miles through the forest preserve until the road terminates at a grassy parking area adjacent to a bend of the river. The 2 miles of the river below Inlet down to the hamlet of Wanakena are not canoeable but are stocked by DEC with brook trout. These miles can be fished successfully from the bank, especially where the river forms a pool. Fly-fishing can be rewarding when the various mayfly hatches are swarming, which is often just before dark. The Royal Coachman is one dry fly frequently used here. The Mickey Finn is a popular streamer pattern. Brown trout, too, are present in this 2-mile stretch of river. In addition to offering exciting fly-fishing opportunities, browns can also be fished with live minnows and with Roostertails, lures which seem to be especially favored locally. The red and white Daredevle also takes many brown trout here.

THE OSWEGATCHIE BELOW CRANBERRY LAKE

Before we talk about the most important part of the Oswegatchie, that section upstream of Inlet, a few words should be said about the river below Cranberry Lake.

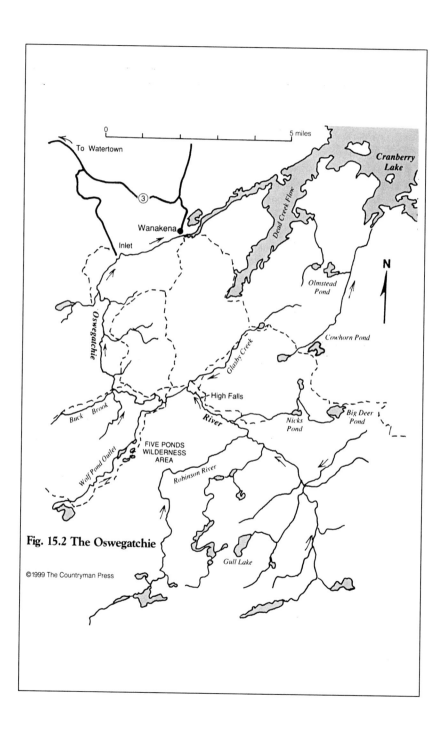

Fig. 15.2 The Oswegatchie

©1999 The Countryman Press

Below the Cranberry Lake dam, the Oswegatchie flows through 8 miles of a timber company tract that is leased to a sportsmen's club. An industrial dam erected still farther downriver at Newton Falls has widened this stretch so that in most areas it resembles a shallow, marshy lake where nesting loons are present. Brook trout and brown trout are stocked annually here by the DEC and are mostly found just below the dam at Cranberry Lake. Smallmouth bass and northern pike lurk in the shallow areas where the water is warmer. Fishing is not prohibited in this stretch. The chief access is from a sandy ramp diagonally opposite the old Cranberry Lake dump on the Tooley Pond Road, approximately ⅔ mile from its intersection with Route 3.

A canoe can be launched here and paddled for a number of miles downriver with a minimum of encumbrances. As the river meanders and widens, numerous weed beds are seen covering the shallows near the shore. A red and white Daredevle cast from a moving canoe or johnboat can often prove irresistible to northerns; 20-pounders have thrilled anglers here on occasion. The Rebel is another effective lure. Both can be used to good effect in late September and October as the fishing for northerns improves. Minnows or small yellow perch used in conjunction with a bobber usually bear fruit to varying degrees throughout the year. The smallmouth bass (along with some largemouth) are frequently taken with minnow-imitating lures.

The April 1 opening of the trout season is quite early for this northern clime. On this date, the lake itself is often still ice clad, while the river is still too cold and too high for the successful pursuit of trout. April 20 to May 1 is usually a more realistic time to begin fishing in this area.

THE OSWEGATCHIE ABOVE INLET

Fishing the Oswegatchie by canoe is generally productive for brook trout for the entire 22 miles above Inlet. At High Falls, a portage is necessary to gain access to the final 7 miles.

As the canoe glides off from the sandy landing, a sense of tranquillity is felt almost immediately. This reflects that the Oswegatchie above Inlet is designated a "wild" river and, as such, motors of any kind are banned. During moderate to high water, the few rapids encountered along the route are navigated fairly easily. At low water, mostly during the summer, a pole can come in handy. You start by paddling upriver against a normally gentle current. However, this current may increase for as much as half a day after heavy rains. The trip downriver usually takes two-thirds the time needed to paddle upstream.

The river meanders slowly, with frequent S-shaped curves giving the paddler ample time to both reflect on the beauty of the surroundings and to cast a worm or lure into the placid waters. (A lure frequently used here is the Panther Martin.) Fishing on the river early in the year can be quite fruitful in the pools lying at the feet of the several rapids. Heading upriver they are Griffin Rapids, Crooked Rapids, and the pool beneath High Falls. Worms and minnows usually work best at this time of year. The trout taken here, while generally small in size, are delicious and can offer a sporting battle.

During the summer, when the water has warmed up considerably, by far the most productive places to cast a line are around the many "spring holes" encountered along the way. These are areas where a true spring bubbles up from the streambed or, more often, where one of the many tributary streams enters the main river. The water stays cooler here during the summer and is far more attractive to trout during this season. These spring holes or tributaries usually are named and well known locally. Going upriver you come across them as follows: Otter Creek, Dorsey Creek, High Rock Creek, Cage Lake Spring Hole, Wolf Creek Spring Hole, and Carter's Landing Spring Hole. Worms and small minnows can still produce here even in summer, but spinners and other lures are used with increasing frequency as the summer progresses.

The river ambles on, framed by an almost continuous canopy of balsam fir, tamarack, and white pine. The white pine in a few cases reaches heroic proportions, some trees exceeding 100 feet in height. After a mile, the river enters an open swamp where, amid thick alders, two of the tributary creeks—Otter Creek on the right and Dorsey Creek on the left—add their measure to the Oswegatchie. These are traditional spring holes but will take some searching to discover as their entrances to the river are fairly well obscured.

After a short stretch in which the river straightens out, the Oswegatchie enters into a large boreal wetland for the next several miles. The river now meanders so extremely that local lore has it that an alert paddler can see the back of his neck. At 4½ miles from Inlet, you'll reach High Rock. This is a huge boulder looking over the wide expanse of wetland just passed through. Primitive camping facilities (including a privy) are located at High Rock; a trail leads from here out to the village of Wanakena in 4 miles. Tiny High Rock Creek comes in here also. It is another of the more prominent spring holes along the river. It was near this spot in 1982 that two DEC forest rangers saw a cow moose and her calf swim across the river, the first indication of breeding success for moose to emerge in more than 100 years in the Adirondacks.

It would be well to mention here that the sights and delights of wildlife add immeasurably to the enjoyment of the entire trip along the river. While there are rivers in the Adirondacks that outstrip the Oswegatchie in the output of trout, few areas surpass it insofar as the quality of wildlife observed and of the wilderness encountered. Therein may lie the ultimate attraction of this small river. Osprey frequently hunt over the river, and often they can be seen plunging in after fish (not trout, we hope!). Loons are often heard, but their calling is from one of the nearby interior ponds—the river itself is too narrow to accommodate them, being only 75 feet at its widest point near Inlet. Broods of mergansers and black ducks are also commonly seen on the river, while great blue herons hunt for frogs in the shallows all along the river's course.

Beaver are abundant on the river and can often be seen swimming alongside the canoe as dusk approaches. Their dams are not much in evidence as they most often use bank dens along the river, especially below High Falls. Otter are also numerous. They occasionally can be observed sticking their heads above the water like seals, but more often you will notice signs of them in the form of slides and rollings in grassy areas on the shore. Whitetail deer are more common here than in many other areas of the Adirondacks. They can frequently be seen feeding on the shores, and the stretch of the river from the plains to High Falls is a large winter deer yard. These upper

Oswegatchie deer are notable both for their size and the imposing girth of many of their racks. Black bear, too, are quite common along the entire length of the river and are occasionally sighted. Much more often bear will make their presence known as they forage for food around the campsite at night. A safety rule when camping along the river is to make sure that all food items are tied high out of the reach of hungry bears and definitely out of the tents.

A short way upstream from High Rock, the river leaves the wide marsh and enters a long, narrow, relatively straight corridor called the Straight of the Woods. The banks are lined here with the cathedral-like spires of balsam fir until the next prominent spring hole is reached, Griffin Rapids, 6½ miles above Inlet. A DEC lean-to is located here, and the first parcel of unharvested or old growth forest is seen on the riverbank. This magnificent stand of sugar maple and beech with an occasional venerable hemlock extends all the way to Buck Pond. The rapids, which are hardly noticeable in medium to high water, provide good fishing (at their heads and also in the pools below) for brook trout of up to 12 inches.

Approximately 8½ miles above Inlet is Cage Lake Spring Hole. A foot bridge spanning the river and a marked trail going to Buck Pond and Cage Lake previously existed here but were recently abandoned by DEC because of the repeated washing out of the bridge in spring floods and incessant beaver flooding of the hiking trail.

In addition to currently being the site of an excellent spring hole, the area is also the site of another DEC lean-to. As is true at all the lean-tos along the Oswegatchie, there is a noticeable paucity of firewood in the immediate vicinity.

Taking off again, the paddler next comes to an imposing stand of large white pine and tamarack lining the river approximately 12 miles above Inlet. The scenery here is, in many respects, more reminiscent of Alaska than New York State. At 12½ miles the one foot bridge still remaining above Inlet is encountered. Crossing the river here is the Five Ponds Trail, which takes you to remote Sand Lake after another 8½ miles of hiking. On the way this trail passes the entrancing Five Ponds themselves, from which the entire Oswegatchie wilderness takes its name. In the vicinity of the five tiny ponds stands a group of magnificent virgin red spruce.

Wolf Creek Outlet is next. This spring hole has produced trout since the days of the early Adirondack guides who had rustic camps in the vicinity. After that, Round Hill Rapids is the next major feature. It and Ross Rapids a little farther upriver are two of the more difficult rapids, and in low water a short carry may be necessary. Fishing for brook trout with worms or minnows at the foot of the rapids is productive during early spring. Another mile on, or about 14 miles upstream of Inlet, yet another notable spring hole is reached: Carter Spring Hole. This name refers to the area between Glasby Creek and Moses Rock Spring, an interval of roughly 100 yards. Glasby Creek drains that unique area known as the Plains, a large open area in a region of otherwise uninterrupted forests. The Plains, which covered the valley between Round Top Mountain and Three Mile Mountain, have only recently begun to revert to forest: black cherry, balsam fir, and tamarack. The Plains, however, retain a generally semi-open aspect.

Finally, 15 miles from Inlet, High Falls is reached. At the foot of the rapids extending from the falls is one of the river's traditional fishing hot spots. The falls have been a prime wilderness destination for nearly a century, going back to the era of Dobson's camps, a popular rustic lodge catering to sportsmen. Nestled under handsome white pine and hemlocks, two other DEC lean-tos are located on either side of the river. Several popular, marked hiking trails also converge here.

Immediately above the falls (after a short carry) the river changes character, becoming more narrow with a deeper channel. The trout get smaller but are still present. More of the trout are now of the native strain, distinguished by salmon-colored flesh, and are excellent eating. On occasion, fly-fishing can be quite exciting above the falls. Fishing into the current is best, and remember that the main hatches of mayflies and stoneflies occur here 10–20 days after the hatches in the southern part of New York State. The Black Gnat is one fly to consider using here. At the confluence of the Oswegatchie and the Robinson Rivers, approximately 3 miles above High Falls, good fishing is provided by the food washed into the Oswegatchie by the

Robinson. Like the spring holes below the falls, fishing in the pool here remains rewarding throughout the summer. The head of navigation is about 6 or 7 miles above the falls, depending on water levels. It is approximately 3 miles to the junction of the Robinson River with two notable spring holes between Nick's Pond outlet and Red Horn Creek.

After 2 miles of paddling, you see a ridge with very large pine on the left. This is known as Pine Ridge and it is an authentic stand of old growth. It was known as the finest example of virgin white pine in the eastern United States before the entire area was decimated by the blowdown of 1950. What remains is still impressive. The best way to see it is to ascend the ridge on an unmarked trail that takes off from an open grassy area on the shore known as Camp Johnny. Camp Johnny is one of the historic primitive campsites located along the river and available for public camping for up to 3 days without a permit.

The Robinson River descends to meet the Oswegatchie next, coming in on a series of rapids approximately a mile after Camp Johnny. Above here the going gets more difficult as the route of the river becomes encumbered with numerous beaver dams and blowdowns. Although the Robinson River is the last traditional spring hole, many small brook trout are still to be found upriver. Fishing for them can be a little difficult with the many alders arching over the river. The trout here are probably best fished for from the many beaver dams that now span the river. This same situation prevails along the lower reaches in areas where small spring creeks enter the Oswegatchie. In many instances the beaver have chosen the exact location where the bodies of water meet to erect the dam, and fishing the pool created by this dam is often good.

Several miles above the Robinson River, the Oswegatchie fans out into various separate feeder creeks and becomes basically unnavigable. Again, though, many of these feeders can be ascended for various lengths depending on water levels. At one time, the pond created by the huge beaver dam near the junction of these feeders was a mecca that beckoned trout fishermen from far and wide. There is still some good trout fishing present here today.

This concludes the Oswegatchie sojourn upriver. The trip

downriver will definitely be quicker and may even reveal some Oswegatchie gems that remained hidden on the upstream paddle.

HEADWATER PONDS

There remains one final fishing opportunity in this fascinating area—the beckoning of the remote headwater ponds. Pursuing the wily trout in these forest-clad bodies of water offers perhaps the zenith in true wilderness fishing. Nestled deep in the forest preserve, they are reached only after long hikes on DEC-marked trails. The way is arduous as the ponds are best fished by boat and the trek in will usually involve taking a lightweight canoe. No matter. Many consider it worthwhile, both for the tranquillity earned and the splendor of the majestic forest traveled through. The difficulty here only enhances the wilderness experience.

Acid rain has affected these interior ponds more than it has Cranberry Lake or the Oswegatchie River. (See the discussion in the introduction.) Those ponds with natural buffering ability have fared best. A number have also been temporarily improved by liming. Most suitable ones have been aerially stocked with brook trout by DEC. Some large trout are still present in these ponds and are best caught by trolling or fly-fishing. Trolling is most productive in early spring, and many trollers favor lures with a worm trailing behind. During warmer weather, the areas of natural springs will have to be sought. The trout will be found congregating there. While increasing acidity has limited the percentage of juvenile fish surviving, 3- and even 4-pound trout are still present in some of these waters as ample reward for the energetic angler who undertakes the long hike back to them.

Following are a sample of some of the ponds that are still moderately productive. While there are others, these will serve quite well as an introduction:

- Cowhorn Pond. This 21-acre pond is reached by a hike of 6½ miles from a trailhead in the hamlet of Wanakena, or, alternatively, by a 4-mile trail from the southwest bay of Cranberry Lake, which can be reached via motorboat.
- Darning Needle Pond. This 30-acre pond can be reached only by a 2½-mile hike on a trail taking off from the south-

east bay of Cranberry Lake. This trip can be done in combination with a day's fishing on Cranberry Lake.

- Tamarack Pond. Comprising 13 acres, this pond is reached by a hike of 8½ miles from the hamlet of Wanakena over the same trail used to reach Cowhorn Pond. In addition, the same alternative exists as at Cowhorn, a 6-mile hike from the trailhead on the southwest bay of Cranberry Lake.

- Hedgehog Pond. This approximately 10-acre pond can be reached after a short ½-mile hike on a trail from the west shore of Cranberry Lake.

Other interior ponds productive for brook trout include Olmstead Pond, the beautiful Five Ponds, and fabled Cage Lake. Cage is reached only after a 9-mile trek from the village of Star Lake or an almost equally lengthy hike from the Oswegatchie River along the marked Five Ponds Trail.

ABOUT THE AUTHOR

A retired police officer, Peter O'Shea is now a naturalist and writer living in New York's St. Lawrence County. He has canoed, trekked, and fished all around the Oswegatchie wilderness country. He is also keenly interested in hunting and cross-country skiing. Peter is the author of several books on hiking in the northern Adirondacks and, in addition, has contributed to a number of magazines. He is a member of the Wildlife Society, the Adirondack Mountain Club, and other groups.

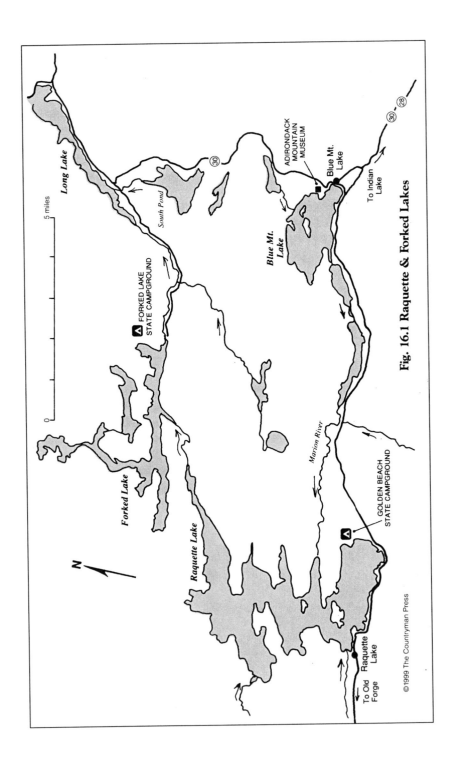

Fig. 16.1 Raquette & Forked Lakes

Long Lake

5 miles

South Pond

30

ADIRONDACK
MOUNTAIN
MUSEUM

Blue Mt.
Lake

30 28

Blue Mt.
Lake

To Indian
Lake

FORKED LAKE
STATE CAMPGROUND

N

Marion River

Forked Lake

Raquette Lake

GOLDEN BEACH
STATE CAMPGROUND

0

Raquette
Lake

To Old
Forge

©1999 The Countryman Press

CHAPTER SIXTEEN

The Raquette River: Highway Through the Mountains

TONY C. ZAPPIA

Stretching from Raquette Lake in central Hamilton County all the way north to its confluence with the St. Lawrence river east of Massena, the Raquette River offers a high-quality and varied outdoor experience. From large, crystal-clear mountain lakes to numerous white-water rapids and easy-flowing stretches of river, the Raquette is readily accessible by motor vehicle yet remote enough to set the stage for a true angling odyssey.

The Raquette undergoes several changes from lake to river along its course. Let's begin our discussion with Raquette Lake, its source.

TROUT AND BASS FISHING IN RAQUETTE LAKE

Raquette Lake's physical features are impressive. It stretches over 5 miles in length and 3 miles in width and has a maximum depth of 96 feet. At 5,274 acres, Raquette is the eighth largest lake in the Adirondacks. It has 99 miles of shoreline and numerous points, inlets, and islands.

As soon as ice-out occurs, brook trout fishing from shore along Route 28 is often very good. Worms seem to be the brookies' favorite meal this time of year, and fish more than 2 pounds are annually weighed in at nearby bait and tackle stores. When the weather warms, brookies will move deeper and may be found near spring holes and cold tributaries.

The second trout indigenous to Raquette Lake is important throughout the Adirondacks: the lake trout. Raquette Lake lakers serve as brood stock insofar as they supply eggs for the Chateaugay Fish Hatchery. At the same time, the Department of Environmental Conservation (DEC) annually stocks the lake with yearling lakers.

A boat is required to fish for lake trout. In the spring, trout can be taken in 30–50 feet of water by trolling flutter spoons with lead core line or copper wire. Downriggers are also used for deep trolling, and lighter line can be used. When concentrating on lakers, it is most important to fish the bottom and fish it slow. Midday (between 10 and 2) often produces the most fish.

As the water warms, lakers find their way to the deeper parts of the lake. At this time, trollers look to the north end, where maximum depth reaches 96 feet. The majority of fish will be found in 35–60 feet, and a depth finder would certainly come in handy to locate fish on the bottom near a structure or, occasionally, suspended.

Bass occupy a different niche here, and they are extremely plentiful. Although bass fishing can be good throughout the summer, Labor Day signals the beginning of cool weather and the best bass-fishing period. Smallmouths and largemouths begin to feed heavily and respond well to bait and lures. Both largemouths and smallmouths congregate along weed beds scattered along the lake, so look for deep water drop-offs that border these weed beds, and drop your offerings into 10–18 feet of water. Minnows and crawfish are the number-one and -two baits. As for lures, Mr. Twisters, Rapalas, and top-water lures such as the Zaraspook, Pop-Rs, buzzbaits, Jitterbug, Hula Popper, and smaller fly-rod poppers can all produce.

While bass and trout fishing may be more exciting, nothing will fill the freezer faster than a couple of days of perch and bullhead fishing. Bullhead can be taken from shore in early spring and fall by fishing mud bottom in 5–15 feet of water. Where you find lily pads along bays, you will usually find perch. Anglers need to offer worms to both perch and bullhead. Under the ice, perch will take a small minnow.

A small boat or canoe is not needed to take pailsfull of bull-head or perch, but for trout and bass fishing, a small- to medium-sized boat is required. A 12- to 16-foot aluminum or fiberglass shallow V-hull is ideal; the motor should be no smaller than 9.9 horsepower. Boat-launching facilities are scattered throughout the town of Raquette Lake. Along Route 28 there are four boat launches that will adequately handle a good-sized craft. Most marinas along the lake will serve the majority of your needs, from bait to boating supplies.

FORKED LAKE

Only ¼ mile from Raquette Lake and part of the same river system, Forked Lake is a medium-sized Adirondack lake spanning 1,248 acres with a maximum depth of 74 feet. Quite rocky, this lake offers both largemouth and smallmouth bass, as well as a good population of brook trout. Both perch and sunfish please the shoreline angler through those hot summer days.

As the days get warmer, brookies will move toward the northwestern part of Forked Lake. Here they will lie in deep holes during the day and move up to the surface at night to take a dry fly, either a real one or one with a hook in it.

Because Forked Lake contains so many rocky shoals and points, the smallmouth bass thrive, and many push the scales to the 4-pound mark. Smallies can be found early in the year along shallow rocky areas with weed beds. It seems as though the fish tend to favor the eastern end of the lake, especially near the outlet waters and near the state campground.

Largemouth bass do well in these waters. Plenty of weed cover offers old bucketmouth plenty of prime locations from which to launch an ambush. To successfully fish largemouths in Forked Lake, one should try rubber worms, spinnerbaits, Mr. Twisters, and various top-water lures. Best bets for locating largemouth are along the east end, where a rock ledge and weed bed are present. Shallow bays make up the west end of the lake, and largemouth are consistently taken here.

The only effective way to fish for bass in Forked Lake is out of a boat. Because the lake is relatively shallow, a boat rigged with an engine larger than 4 or 5 horsepower would be impractical.

Most anglers prefer to use 16-foot canoes or small flat-bottom johnboats. At the Forked Lake Public Campground, anglers can launch a boat and park. There are 78 campsites surrounding the lake. The campsites can be had on a first-come, first-served basis.

Caution: Forked Lake runs west to east and during strong west winds can become quite dangerous for canoeists and others using small craft.

BUTTERMILK FALLS

For those who choose to paddle their way from Forked Lake to Long Lake, the Raquette River drops 116 feet in 5 miles, and three carries must be made to reach the base of Buttermilk Falls. During the spring, brook trout can be taken by fishing at the mouths of feeder streams where they enter the Raquette. Brook trout can also be taken in the Raquette River between Raquette Lake and Buttermilk Falls. A 3-mile section above Buttermilk Falls is annually stocked with brookies during the spring. Worms and spinners work well, but the current will be fairly swift, and pools and eddies will yield the most fish. Canoeists are warned that the rapids above and below Buttermilk Falls are extremely dangerous during high water, and Buttermilk Falls itself is not runnable.

The falls can be reached by motor vehicle from the village of Long Lake by traveling south on Routes 28N/30 and turning right onto North Point Road. Buttermilk Falls parking area is located on the right side of the road and is approximately 5 ½ miles from the center of Long Lake.

THE RAQUETTE RIVER

Anglers fishing out of canoes can resume their journey through the Raquette river system about ¼ mile from the base of Buttermilk Falls. The 4½-mile section of water upriver of the village of Long Lake is scattered with shallow bays of pickerelweed and pond lilies, which are home to great northern pike and both smallmouth and largemouth bass. Anglers who have smaller motorboats in the 14- to 18-foot class can launch at the

Walleyes, like this one of trophy size, are an important part of the menu of a Racquette River float-to-fish trip.

state boat ramp, Town Dock Road, approximately ½ mile from Long Lake Town Beach. Also, there are many private marinas with boat launches along Long Lake where a minimal launch fee will be charged. For the angler without a boat, several places in Long Lake will rent small boats.

LONG LAKE

Long Lake is a fairly shallow, 14-mile-long lake with a maximum depth of 45 feet. Located in northeastern Hamilton County between Routes 28N and 30, the lake is essentially a widening of the Raquette River. It flows roughly south to north, and prevailing summer winds favor downlake travel (south to north).

Northern pike are abundant in Long Lake. Their average weight is 3–4 pounds, although pike in the 10- to 15-pound class can be taken. One of the best areas on the lake for northerns is a place called Big Marsh. Located about 2½ miles north of the village, Big Marsh lies on the western shoreline directly across from Catlin Bay and is defined by a series of marker buoys. Fishermen here cast Daredevles and sinking Rapalas and use live bait early in the morning and later on in the evening. As the water warms, pike will migrate out into the deeper water, and anglers will find them in 15–30 feet. Other hot spots for northerns on Long Lake are the western bays just south of the Long Lake Route 30 bridge and the north marsh at the very foot of Long Lake.

Smallmouth and largemouth bass are concentrated along the north marsh. Because the lake is shallow, the warming of the water tends to play a critical role in fish behavior. Bigger fish will feed heavily at night and in early morning, and fishing Long Lake during midday is generally a waste of time. The only exception is during prespawn conditions. At these times in spring, both pike and bass can be caught any time of day by casting topwater lures close into shore, especially in shallow sandy or weed-filled areas.

When summer arrives, try the deep hole located at the north end of the lake. This 45-foot fish holding area will produce large northerns and bass trying to escape the tepid water temperatures associated with a shallow lake. Recently, a dead pike was discovered floating on top of the water near that area. The fish weighed in at 18 pounds, 12 ounces. If you have a boat equipped with a depth finder, look for suspended fish over deep areas and vertically jig for them. During the early morning and evening hours, concentrate your fishing along structure, such as islands, located adjacent to the 45-foot hole.

Pan fishermen can experience reasonably good perch and bullhead action just about anywhere in the lake. Most panfishing activity occurs around Big Marsh.

Marinas, hotels, stores, and restaurants are primarily located along the eastern shoreline. The south end of the lake is considerably developed, and the north end is mostly forest preserve.

The distance from the village of Long Lake to the north end is 9½ miles. While traveling downlake, you will see lean-tos scattered along the eastern shoreline that are available for use. During peak summer months, lean-tos will become less available because of the hundreds of canoeists traveling through the Raquette River system. If you plan on spending a few days and nights fishing the north end, it would be advisable to carry a tent.

RAQUETTE FALLS

As the river flows out of Long Lake, it forms a marsh, which empties into a slow, winding network of islands and sandbars. A canoe or small motorboat can make its way through this 6-mile-long, slow-moving section of stream until the hills close in as you approach Raquette Falls. You must make a 1⅓-mile carry here in order to continue downstream.

Below (downstream of) the falls, pan-sized brown trout can be taken using worms, spinners, and various fly patterns. Each year, DEC stocks a 1-mile stretch at Raquette Falls. This annual stocking currently takes place by air.

As the river descends some 80 feet, plunging over a rocky bed, the heavy rapids aerate the warm water at the base of the falls. This highly oxygenated water draws both cold- and cool-water species of fish. Your first cast with a crawfish can take a 2-pound brown and your second cast can produce a 24-inch walleye.

The base of Raquette Falls is extremely productive for

northern pike and smallmouth. Walleye averaging 18–24 inches during the spring also find their way to the base of the falls. Both pre- and postspawn walleyes can be tangled with here. Sinking Rapalas, deep-diving crankbaits, spinner/worm combos, or crawfish can draw good responses.

BELOW RAQUETTE FALLS

Still paddling downstream, we come to where the Raquette empties into Tupper Lake (Tupper Lake is discussed in chapter 6). As we leave Tupper Lake and head west on Route 3, we arrive at Piercefield about 7 miles later. Now fully harnessed for generation of hydroelectric power, the river from Piercefield Flow to Raymondville (65 miles downstream) is host to 20 dams and has been nicknamed the "Workhorse River of the North." In spite of this great human intrusion on the lower Raquette, certain fishing opportunities have been created.

Piercefield Flow, the uppermost impoundment on this section of the Raquette, offers fishing opportunities in a pondlike situation. Anglers can take northern pike, smallmouth bass, an occasional walleye, and a variety of panfish. Below Piercefield and downstream to Carry Falls Reservoir is a very wild stretch of the Raquette, one that provides good fishing for smallmouth bass. Although presently used as a canoe route by white-water enthusiasts, the surrounding land is almost entirely private, and access is limited. DEC is presently negotiating to obtain public access along this stretch, but for now, portages around rapids and falls are on private land.

THE RESERVOIRS

For the next 27 miles, beginning with Carry Falls Reservoir, the Raquette is no longer a river; rather, it is a series of eight reservoirs ranging in size from 122 to thousands of acres. Boat launch sites and campgrounds can all be found here. While it varies from reservoir to reservoir, angling is generally good. Walleye, northern pike, yellow perch, smallmouth bass, bullhead, and a variety of other panfish can all be taken in this stretch.

The largest of the reservoirs, Carry Falls—the fifth largest

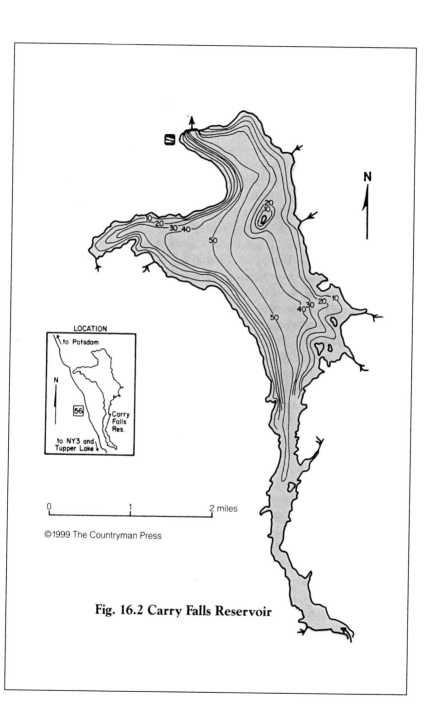

N

0   1   2 miles

©1999 The Countryman Press

Fig. 16.2 Carry Falls Reservoir

lake in the Adirondacks—is located on Route 56 about 3 miles north of Sevey Corners. A blacktop road about a mile long connects this 6⅔-mile-long reservoir with Route 56.

The Parmenter campsite here offers fishermen overnight sites for tents or trailers, as well as picnic tables, toilet facilities, drinking water, and fireplaces. The fee is minimal, and there is no charge for parking or day use.

After camp has been set, you may want to check on water conditions. Water levels can fluctuate as much as 20 feet in Carry Falls, and this will determine the day's fishing activities. As a rule, maximum water level occurs in late April through June, and minimum levels are encountered by late September.

Walleye are the favorite fish, and most anglers troll very slowly with a spinner/worm harness. This is tied to a three-way swivel with either 1 or 2 ounces of weight attached to the system, enabling the rig to bounce bottom. While trolling for walleye it is common to hook into large yellow perch. These tasty fish can reach the 2-pound mark and are abundant here.

The head of Carry Falls Reservoir seems to be a favorite spot with fishermen. Much activity occurs just below the rapids, where water is rich in oxygen and a bit cooler. Early morning and late evening should prove most productive.

Both spring and fall tend to produce the biggest stringers. There are large northern pike cruising the reservoir, so be prepared for bite-offs while fishing for walleye and perch. If you're out after northerns, make sure you spool up with at least 12-pound line, and if possible, tie on a heavier monofilament or wire leader for extra measure.

A word of advice from an old pro who fishes Carry Falls Reservoir: When trolling for walleye, make certain that you troll into the sun for best daytime results.

The final 63 miles of the Raquette winds its way through central St. Lawrence County. It is still flowing essentially northward. The stretch of river from Raymondville to Massena produces good catches of smallmouth bass and walleye. Also, the occasional St. Lawrence River muskellunge can be boated during late spring and fall.

Like an old backcountry road winding its way through the mountains, bending to the left and then to the right, descending down a sloping, hilly, mountain pasture scattered with wildflowers, the Raquette River traverses more than 100 miles of the beautiful Adirondack region. For anglers and other outdoor lovers, it is truly a highway through the mountains.

ABOUT THE AUTHOR

Tony C. Zappia was born and raised in Massena, New York. He is currently a freelance outdoor writer/photographer and outdoor editor for the *Watertown Daily Times*. He is a member of the Outdoor Writers Association of America, the New York State Outdoor Writers Association, and Nikon Professional Services.

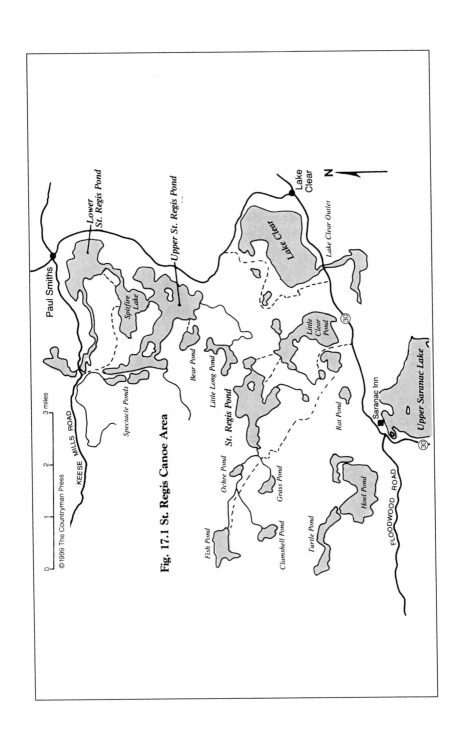

Fig. 17.1 St. Regis Canoe Area

CHAPTER SEVENTEEN

Fishing Pole, Paddle, and Portage

JOE HACKETT

THE ST. REGIS CANOE AREA

The St. Regis Canoe Area is one of the finest places in the Adirondacks to canoe and fish. Located north of the old Remsen–Lake Placid railroad tracks between Paul Smiths and Upper Saranac Lake, the area consists of 58 ponds and lakes, all located on or around the three streams that eventually combine to form the northward-flowing St. Regis River. Within the St. Regis Canoe Area, which is state land open to all, motors of any kind are forbidden. There are several entrances to the area, all of which require portages.

The ponds and lakes of the St. Regis Canoe Area were scooped out by glaciers, and they lie very close together. Most portages are no more than 100 yards and are well maintained by the Department of Environmental Conservation (DEC). All are marked by small white directional signs, and you can easily travel from pond to pond and fish several ponds each day from a base camp. This is the most effective method, as it allows an angler a chance to find which pond is producing on which particular day. Once into the area, a canoeing angler has dozens of options in planning a specific itinerary.

212 Good Fishing in the Adirondacks

Canoeing in to fish the St. Regis area is one of the most popular Adirondack trips. There are dozens of ponds to choose from.

TRAVEL AND FISHING TIPS

Travel in the St. Regis Canoe Area speaks well to the value of a lightweight canoe, and the Kevlar models are the finest. Tugging a heavy aluminum or ABS canoe over a 1-mile-long, buggy, muddy carry is not my idea of a good time. Canoes rigged with oar locks for rowing are a plus. When trolling, it is essential to keep a slow speed to present the bait to the fish, but one must move fast enough to keep the bait from dragging bottom. Rowing allows for greater control, especially in windy conditions.

Trolling methods have proven productive for trout and are easily mastered. Try using a Lake Clear Wabbler with a snelled hook or leader trailing behind. Attach either a night crawler or a streamer fly to the leader. Mickey Finn, Hornberg, Grey Ghost, and Muddler Minnow are popular patterns for streamers. Trolling a streamer without the Wabbler requires that the fisherman twitch or sweep the rod to cause the streamer to dart like a wounded minnow. Real minnows are not allowed as bait in any of the St. Regis Canoe Area ponds, as some of the ponds have been reclaimed to clean out all the junk fish.

Rods should be medium action with 6- to 8-pound-test lines for trolling. Ultralight spinning rods with 4-pound-test lines are good for casting. Fly rods should be 7½ to 8½ feet in length and should take a 6- to 7-weight line; a sinking-tip line is useful for trolling. Fly hatches are numerous and are similar to most Adirondack river hatches. The peak of the mayfly hatches is late May through early June, but sporadic hatches occur throughout the season. Using dry flies like a Black Gnat or Adams in size 14 or 16 at dusk is often productive. Lakers have been known to feed heavily on the surface late in the day, and casting a size 6–8 White Wulff or Rat Faced MacDougal will sometimes result in furious action. A favorite technique is to drift the shorelines of these ponds and cast small ⅛- to ¼-ounce spinning lures along the shore. Look for schools of fleeing minnows along the shore early and late in the day, and cast the lure in front of them. A slow retrieve with a twitch of the rod every few revolutions has taken many nice fish. Many lures will work, but good results are often had with Phoebes, Mepps, C.P. Swings, and Kastmasters, in gold or brass tone.

STARTING OUT

There are two public boat launch/parking areas at the eastern end of the St. Regis Canoe Area. One is located on Little Clear Pond, behind the Saranac Inn State Fish Hatchery off Route 30; no fishing is allowed in Little Clear Pond as it is a brood pond for landlocked salmon. Access to St. Regis Pond, the largest pond in the area, is made via a 2-mile paddle up Little Clear Pond, then a ¼-mile carry. The other launching site is located off Route 30 on Upper St. Regis Lake, next to the private Lake Shore Owners Association's boathouse and docks. This site requires a ½-mile paddle across the Upper St. Regis Lake and several short carries through Bog Pond, Bear Pond, and Little Long Pond.

The western end of the St. Regis Canoe Area is accessible off the Floodwood Road, 4 miles west of the state hatchery on Route 30. The Floodwood Road divides the St. Regis Canoe

Area from the Fish Creek–Rollins Pond Camping Areas. It is also the dividing line between cold-water and cool-water game-fish species. For access to this section of the St. Regis Canoe Area, a state launch is located on Hoel Pond, adjacent to the Saranac Inn Golf Course. Putting in on Hoel Pond requires a paddle of 2 miles across the pond and a carry over the railroad tracks and into Turtle Pond. From Turtle Pond, one can paddle into Slang Pond and carry over to Long Pond or carry 1 mile directly into Clamshell Pond. From Clamshell, a half-mile carry leads to Fish Pond.

Long Pond, which has a state launch on its western end, can be accessed via the Floodwood Road just past the West Pine Pond turnoff. Long Pond has a decent population of small-mouth bass and is a starting point for trips to Ledge Pond, which holds lake trout, brook trout, and lots of perch. Also accessible from Long Pond are carries to Mountain Pond (brook trout) and the trail to Nellie and Bessie Ponds, which requires a mile-long carry. Fishing the ledges along the narrows on Long Pond always produces some nice smallmouth bass.

THE EAST END

The St. Regis Canoe Area can be best described in two sections: the East End and the West End.

The East End is centered around St. Regis Pond. It holds a good population of lake trout (18-inch minimum size limit), splake, and brook trout. It is best fished on calm days, as the wind can make for rough water because of the size of the pond. Trolling shorelines or casting spinners along the shore of the big island on St. Regis Pond is a good bet in the early season. As the heat of the summer intensifies, fish deep, using copper or lead core line about 50 yards off the island. The East End of the canoe area also holds Little Long Pond, Grass Pond, Little Clear Pond (no fishing), Bear Pond, Bog Pond, Ochre Pond, Green Pond, Meadow Pond, and St. Germain Pond. Nearly all of these little jewels hold brook trout, some lake trout, splake, and rainbows. Little Long Pond is well known for the latter three. Fly hatches are common in these stone-bottom ponds and are very noticeable on Little Long Pond in May and June. The dimples on the water at dusk will make any fly fisherman smile.

Try trolling or casting spinners along the east shore of Green Pond, especially around the downed trees. Another hot spot is along the small island on Little Long Pond, often a favorite location for shore fishermen who angle for rainbows throughout the evening. The fishing remains good on these ponds because of substantial stocking by DEC. The East End of the St. Regis Canoe Area does, however, see a lot of traffic. It is very popular with day-tripping canoeists, and holiday weekends can be very crowded. Overfishing in the early season can reduce fish populations, so catch-and-release fishing is stressed. Keep only enough for the evening meal, and you're sure to be rewarded in the future.

THE WEST END

The west end of the St. Regis Canoe Area is centered on two large bodies of water. Long Pond, which has been mentioned, offers access to Ledge Pond, Mountain Pond, Slang Pond, Turtle Pond, Ebony Pond, Track Pond, and Hoel Pond. Hoel Pond, Ledge Pond and Long Pond are known for big lake trout. The others hold decent populations of brook trout. Between Long Pond and St. Regis Pond lies the other big pond in the area, Fish Pond, with its two lean-tos on opposite shores. The tranquillity this woodland pond offers is the reward most brook trout fishermen seek; the fishing is a bonus. Fish Pond is surrounded by Nellie, Bessie, Kit Fox, Mud, Little Long, Little Fish, Lydia, and Clamshell Ponds and offers more solitude than any of the other large ponds in the area. It is arduous getting to Fish Pond, and that tends to keep the day-trippers at bay.

The ponds surrounding Fish Pond all hold good populations of brook trout, with Nellie, Bessie, and Clamshell Ponds clear favorites. Fishing pressure at this end of the area is heavy at times, particularly in the spring and fall. Fish Pond also produces some nice lake trout, along with a generous number of brook trout. The shoals along the west end of Fish Pond offer particularly good opportunities for lake trout in the spring. This is certainly a place to practice catch and release. Take a couple of nice fish for dinner, and toss the rest back for future fishing fun. Bullheads, a fine eating fish, are plentiful in nearly all the ponds in the St. Regis Area and can be caught all night long with a hook, sinker, and worm that is cast out and left on the bottom.

THE FISH CREEK AREA

Adjacent to the St. Regis Canoe Area, but on the south side of the railroad tracks, is the Fish Creek–Rollins Pond State Campsite. The Fish Creek area offers some outstanding fishing opportunities for both cool-water and cold-water species. The state campgrounds on Fish Creek and Rollins Pond are well kept and operated by DEC. They offer a fine base camp area for day trips to the many ponds surrounding this area. Boats with motors are allowed in many of these ponds, and access is often right off Route 30. The fishing opportunities for smallmouth and largemouth bass are excellent, and there are enough northern pike available to make things interesting.

Some of the better cool-water ponds are Follensby, Clear (off Route 30), Copperas, Square, Rollins, and Fish Creek Ponds. One pond that has consistently produced nice catches of bass and northern pike is Floodwood Pond. Easily accessed via the Floodwood Road off Route 30 at Saranac Inn, the pond can offer some furious smallmouth fishing with surface poppers. It is one of the prime heat-of-the-summer bass ponds in this area. The action trollers experience with northerns can also be surprising, especially at the western end of the pond near the channel to Rollins Pond. Fish surface poppers or other lures along the shoreline wherever you find downed trees and stumps. These ponds all feed into the Upper Saranac Lake, and many primitive campsites are located on the shores.

Boat and canoe rentals are also located nearby at Hickok Boat Livery on Fish Creek Pond. Numerous roadside ponds are located in this area, and some hold decent populations of brook trout and rainbows. Whey Pond in the Fish Creek Campsite is a special-trout-regulations water (minimum length 12 inches, three fish per day, artificials only). It is known for its trophy rainbows and brook trout. Black Pond, located nearby, is also a good bet. Horseshoe, Sunrise, Echo, Rat, and Sunday Ponds round out the list of brooktrout ponds.

BASS FISHING

Bass fishing has been overlooked in the Adirondacks, mainly because trout and salmon are so readily available. The cool-water fisheries of the Fish Creek–Saranac Area are ideal bass habitat, as are Upper and Lower St. Regis Lakes and Meacham Lake. The shorelines of these waters offer rocky shoals and numerous downed trees. This spells structure, and bass love it. Other than a large salmon, there is nothing I'd rather have on the end of a fly rod than a scrappy smallmouth bass. At the end of a hot summer day, smallmouth action can be outstanding. Using a small cork popper on a fly rod or a surface lure on a spinning rod, fish close to the shorelines of the ponds. The closer you can cast to the shore, right in among the weeds and limbs, the better your chances. As the water calms toward dusk, the big fish are often taken in the shallow areas near drop-offs to deep water. Bass in the 2- to 3-pound range are available, and the occasional northern pike will often boil out of the water for a surface plug. Best choices are cork poppers with rubber legs in green, black, or yellow, or surface Rapalas, Rebels, and frog imitations. Fishing crankbaits or leadhead jigs with rubber worms in the deeper water will produce fish in the heat of the day. Minnows either trolled or cast with a bobber to shore will do well, especially for pike. Unfortunately, most pike will take live bait deep, making releasing fish difficult. Although minnows produce well, so many small pike are killed in the releasing of them that minnows should be reserved as a last resort when all else fails.

THE BOG RIVER FLOW WILDERNESS AREA

An area that rivals the St. Regis Canoe Area for beauty and solitude is the Bog River Flow Wilderness Area. Located in St. Lawrence County, just west of Tupper Lake, this area is accessed via Route 471 off Route 30 south of Tupper Lake. The turnoff to Horseshoe Lake–Veterans Mountain Camp leads around

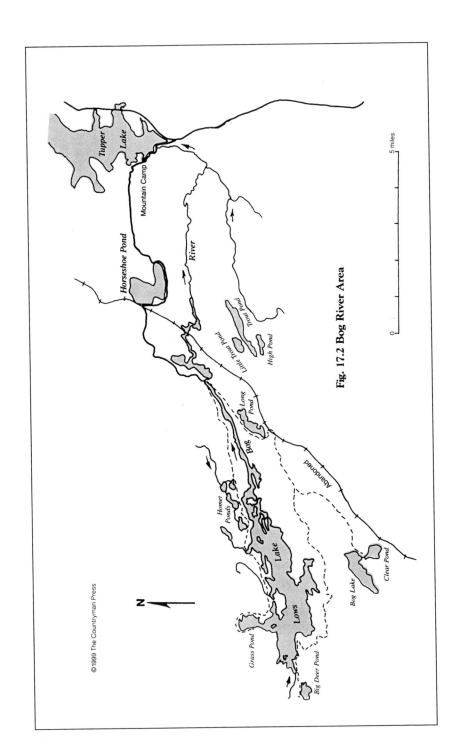

Fig. 17.2 Bog River Area

Horseshoe Lake 6 miles to a dirt road that dead-ends at the state launch on the lower dam of the Bog River. This large tract includes the Bog River Flow, which connects Hitchins Pond, Lows Lake, Grassy Pond, Tomar Pond, and several other natural ponds, which were back flooded as a result of the creation of the upper dam on Lows Lake. A very large, but quite shallow body of water, with an average depth of 8–10 feet, Lows Lake is very susceptible to heavy waves. Even with a light wind the lake can whitecap, and with the prevalent western winds not blocked by any large mountains, Lows Lake can often be unnavigable by canoe.

The launch at the lower dam leads one upriver 2 miles to Hitchins Pond. Another shallow body of water, Hitchins rarely gets as rough as Lows Lake. It contains brook trout, bass, and yellow perch; however, the trout are only fishable in the very early season. As soon as the water warms enough for the perch to become active, an angler cannot get through the perch to get at the brookies. The perch, some as large as 1½ pounds and 16 inches long, can provide plenty of action for the kids, and if prepared as "poor man's shrimp," they make a wonderful meal for adults. They are easily caught on spinners or hook and worm.

A short carry at the head of Hitchins Pond leads over the upper dam and into Lows Lake. The first 7 miles up the flow are quite narrow and not often windy. Once you get past the Boy Scout Camp on the right shore, the lake begins to widen until a second narrow passage is reached about 1 mile farther along. Once through this channel, a view of Lows Lake proper is achieved, and you are greeted with the usual whitecapped waves. Lows Lake is speckled with several beautiful islands, but camping is limited to a few numbered sites. The majority of the island campsites are reserved for Boy Scout use in June, July, and August.

Grassy Pond, located near the head of Lows Lake, offers true remoteness and a feeling of real wilderness. Grassy Pond Mountain, with its soaring cliffs, is a known nesting site for bald and golden eagles. Eagles are often spotted on Lows Lake, along with large numbers of loons, which breed in this area. Coyotes and owls usually are heard during the evening, and moose have been spotted in the area.

The fishing in Lows Lake, Grassy Pond, and the Bog River is not as good as it used to be for brook trout. Bass were introduced in the early 1980s and have nearly displaced brook trout throughout this waterway. Because the wind is so often a problem, trolling can be difficult, but it is effective. Spinners cast along shorelines can produce nice catches, as can poppers or jigs. Best bets are to cover shorelines in stumpy areas or along the cobblestoned islands. Trout seem to slack off by late June as the water warms but pick up again in September.

I find that trout fishing on the lakes and ponds falls into several distinct time frames in regards to peak production. Ideally, the best time to fish brook trout is right after the ice goes off the pond. Generally, this is late April or early May in the northern Adirondacks, but the amount of snowfall and extremes of winter temperatures affect ice-out dates drastically. In a 5-year span, ice-out on the ponds has ranged from March 28 to May 7. Predicting the day the ice will go is difficult at best; even so, the first weekend in May is often a safe bet for good fishing.

Brook trout feed heavily and respond favorably to just about anything tossed their way for the first week to 10 days after ice-out. Unfortunately, this feeding frenzy leads into what I call the "2-week doldrums." Some ponds may produce for 2 days after ice-out, some as long as 10 days. But after this initial strong feeding period, the trout can then go off their feed for as long as 2 weeks. The end of the doldrums is marked by the first few hatches of the season and is over for sure once the dragonfly nymphs are out.

Consistently, Mother's Day weekend in early May has produced the finest fishing of the year. Hatches continue throughout May and June, and the trout remain on the feed. As the heat of the summer comes upon the ponds, the water warms and trout seek deeper, cooler water. Often they congregate in the spring holes or in the area of feeder streams on the ponds. Usually, the depth of the water the fish are in negates trolling, so still fishing is the order of the day. July and August bring the hottest weather, and trout fishing is reduced to early morning or early evening trips in search of rising trout. This period need not be a fishless one, however, as bass and pike can be taken readily in deep water during the day and along the shoreline at dusk. The trout fishing picks up in September and is very good as the cool fall nights lower the water temperature. A fat fall brook trout in spawning colors offers a splendid complement to the spectacular autumn foliage. The warm days and cool nights make for enjoyable camping, and there are no bugs and fewer people in the woods after Labor Day.

ABOUT THE AUTHOR

Joe Hackett has owned and operated Tahawus Guide Service since 1978. He grew up in Elizabethtown, New York, fishing the Boquet River. After earning a master's degree in recreation and outdoor education in 1980, Joe cofounded the New York State Outdoor Guides Association. Today he specializes in fly-fishing remote ponds for brook trout. The St. Regis Canoe Area is one of the regions he knows best. He lives in Ray Brook with his wife and two little girls.

FOOTNOTE: LAKES IN THE BIG WOODS

LITTLE TUPPER LAKE

Little Tupper Lake is part of the 1998 state land purchase. It lies within the William C. Whitney Area and is the home to the Little Tupper strain of brook trout. Little Tupper can be accessed from the Circle Road (Highway 10A) roughly 7 miles north of Long Lake village. There's a boat launch (no motors allowed) below the forest ranger base (formerly Whitney Headquarters).

Little Tupper is shallow for a brook trout lake, with only two deep holes: one 37 feet, the other 18 feet. The best fishing is the first couple of weeks after ice-out and in September. Little Tupper, as of this writing, is strictly catch-and-release fishing.

LAKE LILA

Eight miles beyond the forest ranger base, at the end of a 5 ½-mile drive down a dirt road, sits the Lake Lila parking area. There is a ¼-mile portage to the lakeshore put-in. Like Little Tupper, no motors are allowed on Lake Lila, but the lake is not strictly catch and release. The Lake Lila parking area holds only

30 cars, so if it is filled, you must park on the Sabattis Road and carry your canoe the 5½ miles; all land on each side of the dirt road is private.

Beautiful Lake Lila has good fishing for landlocked salmon (stocked), lake trout, and brook trout in the spring, and small-mouth bass during the warm months. Camping is allowed on four of the seven islands. There are also designated campsites on the mainland.

STILLWATER RESERVOIR

Stillwater Reservoir is a sizable backwater created by the dam-ming of the Beaver River, which flows out of Lake Lila. Stillwater has some excellent smallmouth bass fishing and is also stocked with splake. There are some lake trout and brook trout as well.

The big reservoir is a fairly remote destination, and just get-ting to it can be an adventure. From Eagle Bay in the Fulton Chain, turn north off Route 28 onto the Big Moose Road. After a little more than 6 miles, turn left at what is called Glenmore Corner, and continue on 1½ miles to Big Moose. The hardtop ends here. It is 10 more miles to the Stillwater Road, where you turn into the forest ranger headquarters and the boat launch.

—Dennis Aprill

CHAPTER EIGHTEEN

The St. Lawrence River

ALLEN BENAS

Serving as the common border between the United States and Canada for just more than 100 miles, the St. Lawrence River has beckoned to freshwater anglers in both nations for centuries. The majestic river, at 568 miles, is one of the longest in the continental United States and provides year-round fishing enjoyment for the whole family. The St. Lawrence River is named after the saint honored on the day of its discovery in 1615. It stretches from its source, the eastern end of Lake Ontario, northeasterly to the Gulf of St. Lawrence.

The river's recreational area is contained within the first 90 miles, from Lake Ontario to Massena, New York. From the beautiful village of Massena downstream, the river is little more than a ditch as it leads to Montreal, Quebec City, and on to the Gulf. At its source at Lake Ontario, the river is more than 20 miles across. Dotted here by more than 1,700 islands of every size and description, it gradually narrows to only a few miles wide in its first 35 miles of flow. This expanse of water misled the earliest French explorer, Jacques Cartier, to name the region Lac Des Mille Isles, or Lake of the Thousand Islands. It is this section, now an extremely popular vacation and resort region, that has established the river as an angler's paradise.

The St. Lawrence Seaway has been referred to as one of the most dramatic engineering undertakings of the century. With its completion in 1959, this conduit to the sea helped create the longest inland waterway on our planet. Ships from around the world now penetrate half a continent, while power generated by the great river supplies vast areas of both New York State and the Canadian province of Ontario. From the standpoint of international commerce, the seaway opened the Great Lakes to direct oceangoing shipping traffic, linking all ports along the lakes—as far west as Duluth, Minnesota—to world markets. But environmentally, the seaway has been described by many as the worst thing that ever happened to the Great Lakes and St. Lawrence River—as it soon became clear that the benefits of world commerce did not come without cost.

At first, it was pollution. Ships discarded everything—ballast water taken on in the world's ports, garbage, and even bilge sludge and oil—into the river. Sewage too was a problem, as holding tanks were unheard of back then. As with our own US and Canadian industry, the ships looked on our river and lakes as receptacles for any and all kinds of refuse and processing wastes. Environmental laws and strict enforcement have long since put a stop to these infractions, and the water now runs clean, clear, and surprisingly pure.

Most recently, the introduction of little mollusks called zebra mussels have further changed the water conditions. These were introduced in ballast water discharged from freighters entering the system from the Black Sea and proliferated at astonishing rates. Water once clouded by plankton is now crystal clear as each mussel filters as much as two liters of water a day. Where visibility was once limited to only a few feet, bottom is now visible as deep as 40 feet in early spring and late fall. Fortunately, nature has corrected for the imbalance by generating increased plankton hatches during the warmest months, allowing small fish to survive until their diet becomes smaller fish.

Weed growth has also changed. What were once huge weed beds dotting the river in depths of as much as 20 feet are now gravel bars littered by empty clam shells. Elsewhere in the river is a new kind of vegetation that accumulates in great masses of slippery, slimy weeds that look and feel like silk. As described by one botanist, the river is going through a transformation.

To those simply intent on having an enjoyable vacation, the river offers unmatched scenic beauty, unlimited cruising oppor-

Giant muskies like this still swim in the St. Lawrence, where Arthur Lawton once took freshwater angling's most revered record: a monster muskellunge 1 ounce short of 70 pounds.

tunities, the certainty of catching fish, and a relaxed lifestyle that is unmatched by more confined and crowded vacation areas. To professional angling organizations such as the Bass Anglers Sportsmen's Society, the river holds more bass per acre than most places they conduct tournaments. To muskie hunters the world over, the river is considered Mecca. A world-record muskie was taken here in 1957 that reigned uncontested for 35 years.

Although populated by a wide array of freshwater fish, the river's reputation as a premier sport fishery focuses on four major species: great northern pike, smallmouth bass, walleye, and muskellunge. Seasons for these vary, so anglers can be on the river from early May through mid-March. As the river begins to run fresh in the spring, usually in early April, fishermen anxiously await the opening of the northern pike season on the first Saturday in May. The success on opening day will depend heavily on what kind of spring the area had. A cold spring can set back the spawn, meaning that the mature pike could still be in the shallows of the marshes, safe from the angler's lure. A warming or "normal" spring beginning in early April means business as usual.

Although it is an immense water area, the St. Lawrence attracts boats of every size. Given calm winds and a sense of stable weather, anglers in boats as small as 14 feet are a common sight. Should the wind increase, the numerous islands offer shelter, and the waters surrounding them can be productive.

PIKE

Knowledgeable pike anglers will seek out locations where they know there is underwater weed growth. With recent changes in the marine ecology, this knowledge is based on fishing experience during recent summers, when weed beds still grow to the surface. The alternative is to fish much deeper in search of trophy pike that seek shelter from bright light in the river's depths and bottom growth.

The northern pike prefers to lie in hiding, awaiting the unsuspecting passerby. Like other members of the *Esox* genus, the pike is an ambush hunter. The most successful pike anglers will use large silver shiners, available locally (although imported from Arkansas). They are usually drifted just off the river bottom. Seldom will a pike pass up an opportunity for this tender morsel. Often, deep-running artificial lures are productive. Daredevle spoons, deep-running crankbaits, and jigs with worm and twister tails (either pork or plastic) have established reputable stature in the angler's northern pike arsenal.

Use ultralight to medium-weight tackle for pike. A good bet for a sporting encounter would be a light-action rod and reel with a capacity for at least 175 yards of 6-pound monofilament line. A stronger leader is suggested, not so much for pulling strength as for protection from pikes' ultrasharp teeth.

Well-traveled anglers often compare northern pike fishing in the St. Lawrence with other areas. The consensus is that larger fish, although in smaller numbers, can still be caught farther north, in Canada. But when it comes to quantity, the St. Lawrence shines. Limit catches with an average size of 4–5 pounds (with occasional trophies in the 10- to 15-pound class) are the rule.

Northern pike are a popular attraction for ice fishermen from freeze-up (usually in early January) until the season closes in March. Specimens as large as 20 pounds are not unheard of during the winter months, when the largest pike of the year are usually caught.

Popular wintertime northern pike hangouts can be found at Wilson Hill Causeway between Louisville and Massena off Route 37B; Coles Creek Marina between Waddington and Massena on Route 37; Brandy Brook, just east of Waddington on Route 37; the pulp docks in Ogdensburg (east of old Diamond National Plant); Perch Bay outside Morristown off Route 37; and Chippawa Bay.

Early-season, open-water pike fishing can also be quite good in the waters mentioned, as they will produce numerous post-spawn fish. Often overlooked, boat marinas offer outstanding early-season pike fishing. You can find marina facilities in nearly every community along the St. Lawrence. The season for northern pike extends from early May through March 15 of the following year. It then closes for 7 weeks to allow for the spawn. The pike season is the longest of all sportfishing seasons on the river.

SMALLMOUTH BASS

It is hard to say which fish is synonymous with the St. Lawrence: the muskie or the smallmouth bass. But there is no doubt that the smallmouth is far more abundant, being found in large numbers from Cape Vincent to Massena. No native needs a calendar to tell when the third Saturday in June has arrived. This is the heaviest-traffic day of the year, with cars, vans, campers, and boat trailers all heading for the river. Ask any old-timer along the river when the tourist season starts, and he'll more than likely say, "When the bass season opens!" Many things make bass the most sought after of all the river species. Above all, they are spectacular fighters. Pound for pound, they are the fightingest fish that swims, as the expression goes.

Throughout the summer months bass will move constantly, from day to day, even hour to hour. Weather fronts will affect them more than other species, as will sunlight and cloud cover. One day they will be deep, the next, shallow. You might catch them in 20 feet in the morning but have to go down 120 feet in the afternoon. Any self-professed bass expert you hear about along the St. Lawrence is probably giving himself a lot more credit than he should. Bass, simply put, are intimidating fish; they can make fools out of the best anglers. That's probably the main reason sportsmen love to go after them.

The St. Lawrence Valley was created by glaciation eons ago, during the ice ages. Consequently, there is no such thing as an average depth. With the deepest spot being nearly 300 feet, with adjacent islands only a few yards away, you can appreciate how a 30-foot boat can have its bow in one foot of water while anglers fish in 25 feet off the stern. Where modern crankbaits, for example, may serve well in impoundments, we have found it impossible to get them down to the 50-plus-foot depths that hold bass during the hot summer months.

Early in the season, while bass are still in the shallows, artificials can be very effective. After they move into deeper water, artificials are most practical in the evenings, when the bass move into the shallows to feed. Successful casting of artificials is done in depths ranging from a few to no more than 15 feet of water. Evening casting is best in bays or along the shoreline and around docks. The most popular artificials among visiting pros are jig-and-pig, medium-sized spinnerbaits, and small crankbaits.

As with pike fishing, the most successful anglers will use shiners. These 2- to 3-inch long bait fish will produce more fish than all lures combined. Think of it this way: How can you improve on the fish's natural food?

As for pike, the best tackle for bass ranges from ultralight to medium weight. A good bet for a sporting encounter would be a light-action rod and reel with a capacity for at least 175 yards of 6-pound monofilament line.

Favorite smallie waters along the St. Lawrence can be found starting near Cape Vincent midway up the north side of Grenadier Island (especially after a north wind); the shoal on the northwest corner between Haddock and Grenadier Island (good late-summer fishing); Wilson Bay (south of Tibbetts Point Lighthouse); and the waters between Fox Island and the mainland. Moving east (downstream), numerous shoals and weed beds along Clayton and Alexandria Bay hold large populations of bass.

Farther downriver, smallmouth bass can be found along any current break or weed bed between Morristown, Ogdensburg, Waddington, Louisville, and Massena. Pike and bass remain the most popular of the St. Lawrence fishes throughout the summer months.

MUSKIE

As mid-September approaches with its shorter days and cooler nights, there is another group of anglers who begin to appear on the scene. Decked out in heavy garb, braving the chilled river in boats ranging in size from 16–25 feet, these anglers are in search of the ultimate freshwater trophy. These are the muskie hunters.

To some, the muskie is the fish of 10,000 casts; to others, the fish of 1,000 hours. To no one is it an easy gamefish. What makes the St. Lawrence still a choice muskie fishing destination? One reason may be that it holds the largest of the two remaining natural, or unstocked, strains of muskellunge left in North America. Another may be the knowledge that a world-record muskie came from this water. It was "on Sunday morning September 22 [1957]," the late Arthur Lawton wrote in his chronicle of the great fish in the June 1958 issue of *Outdoor Life*, "trolling off a small grassy island a few miles below Clayton, I hung and boated the biggest muskellunge ever landed on hook and line, a fish that on Monday evening, 30 hours after it was caught, weighed in at 69 pounds, 15 ounces—4 ounces heavier than the previous world record."

But anglers don't come to the river as intent on breaking Lawton's record as they are on setting their own. Perhaps they are after their first legal-sized fish, a personal record in itself. Maybe a 30-plus-pounder is what they're after—small perhaps in comparison to Lawton's, but a very respectable trophy nevertheless. All of these are records when you are a muskie hunter.

The range of the St. Lawrence muskie, both as a species and individually, is the largest of all river gamefish. They are found everywhere between Lake Ontario and Massena. The three most popular areas, however, remain the Thousand Islands region (where Lawton's record fish fell), around the city of Ogdensburg, and below the village of Massena.

In 1984 a study to learn more about the unique St. Lawrence River strain of muskellunge was initiated by the SUNY College of Environmental Science and Forestry at Syracuse. Netting in suspected spawning locations yielded several specimens. While most were scale-sampled, tagged, and released, nearly 2 dozen were fitted with small external transmitters. These radiotelemetry devices allowed biologists to trace the movements of the muskies in this vast waterway. What the biologists found was previously unsuspected by all but a few experienced muskie fishing guides. St. Lawrence River muskies are travelers; they are migratory. Mature fish tend to spawn in the same bays every year, but after the spawn they leave the area for larger ranges. Most Thousand Islands muskies summer in Lake Ontario. Fish that winter in Ogdensbury summer in the Thousand Islands, a much larger area of the river 60 miles upstream.

Part of the muskellunge strategy is timing. Most muskie fishing is done in the fall. The fish are at the height of their aggressiveness, gorging themselves in anticipation of lean winter months that lie ahead. Muskie mania prevails along the St. Lawrence from mid-September until the season closes on November 31. By far, the vast majority of muskies are taken by trolling. Large lures are trolled at speeds that make them perform at the peak of their intended design. Many veteran muskie anglers will tell you "it doesn't make much difference if the lure moves like a fish, as long as it moves like it's crazy." Every seasoned muskie fishermen I know contends that the color of a lure is secondary. It is the action that drives them nuts, and nutty fish make mistakes. The most successful lures have two or three sections and are 6–9 inches long. For years the majority of muskies were taken on the then-popular Creek Chub lures, which worked well with the heavy Monel line that was used to get the lures down to depths of 20 feet. With the gaining popularity of downrigger fishing, allowing for much lighter tackle and thus more sport, these have now been replaced in popularity and performance by a multisectioned lure manufactured by the Radtke Bait Company. Although this lure takes most Thousand Islands muskies, lures such as the Believer, Cisco Kid, Rapala, and Water Dog work well on downriggers and chalk up success year in and year out.

Among the most popular muskie fishing spots along the St. Lawrence are the waters off Cape Vincent, including Featherbed and Hinkley Shoals. Downriver toward Clayton, anglers congregate on the famous 40-Acre Shoals, Gananoque Narrows, and just west of the international bridge in the fast-flowing water adjacent to the shipping channel. Still farther downstream, the area around Chippewa Bay, although treacherous to even experienced boaters, is a known muskie hangout. Below Chippewa Bay you enter the Brockville Narrows, where muskie fishermen also converge. At Ogdensburg, most muskie fishing activity focuses on the sandbar where the Oswegatchie River empties into the St. Lawrence, just upstream from the international bridge. This is the only place along the entire river where most fishing is done at night. This rare occurrence stems from not only the movements of the fish (which come in to feed when the sun goes down) but also from the fact that the more prominent guides have day jobs and can only fish at night. Regardless, night-fishing here produces.

The farthest east that muskie fishing is done is in Lake St. Lawrence, both above and below the St. Lawrence/Franklin Delano Roosevelt Power Dam located just outside Massena. Above the dam muskie fishermen concentrate their activities near Coles Creek, Wilson Hill, and Long Sault Islands. Below the dam most muskie hunters key in on the tail race on the American side. Here numerous muskies are caught and released on a regular basis. Trolling one or two lures per angler, depending on whether you are fishing in Ontario or New York waters, fishermen follow underwater contours in depths ranging from 18 to as deep as 60 feet.

In recent years muskie fishing has improved dramatically. Many attribute the increased catches, particularly in the 40-plus-pound class, to the catch-and-release efforts started back in the early 1980s. Others contend that it is a combination of that and nature's evolutionary cycle, resulting in both good and bad hatch years. Regardless, days can be spent with not even a hit.

On the other hand, occasionally a boat will limit out in only a few hours. Most dedicated muskie hunters do agree on one thing: In comparison to muskie fishing, a crapshoot is a sure thing!

WALLEYE

In addition to the species already mentioned, the upper St. Lawrence also holds a promising population of walleye. Because of a lack of angler pressure, walleyes have been allowed to multiply and grow to record-class size. Seven- and 8-pounders are average here, and 12- to 15-pounders are trophies (when is the last time you threw back a 6-pound walleye?).

The most successful spring walleye fishing is done in shallow bays in May and June by those casting Rapalas, small crankbaits, and jigs tipped with worms. During late July and August most activity is between the shipping channel and adjacent shallower areas, where the fish are intercepted with jigs and night crawlers as they head in to the shallows to feed in the dark. The most popular walleye spots are Carleton Island, near Cape Vincent, New York, and Fishers Landing, New York, just west of the Thousand Islands Bridge.

The mouth of the Oswegatchie River in Ogdensburg has started producing good catches of walleye. Within the past few years, the waters between Waddington and Massena have also produced outstanding catches of large walleye. Of course, one of the premier walleye fishing grounds is below the St. Lawrence/FDR Power Dam. Here fishing is done exclusively from boats. Most walleye are concentrated in the tail race of the dam, and early morning and early evening seem to be the best times. For nonangling members of the family, dozens of attractions will provide hours and even days of activity while the anglers enjoy their sport. The St. Lawrence River makes the area an international playground shared by Americans, Canadians, and visitors from around the world. They come to cruise, and they come to camp. Many come for the numerous attractions. But by far, most come to fish the waters of the bountiful boundary.

ABOUT THE AUTHOR

Allen Benas is a member of the Outdoor Writers Association of America, the New York State Outdoor Writers Association, and the Pennsylvania Outdoor Writers Association. He has served as president of the Clayton–Thousand Islands Chamber of Commerce, charter member and first chairman of the Jefferson County Sport Fishery Advisory Board, member of the Fishery Committee of the International Joint Commission on the Great Lakes, and president of the Clayton Guides Association.

Benas has lived in the Thousand Islands section of the St. Lawrence River since 1950. He and his wife have operated the Thousand Islands Inn in Clayton, New York, since 1973. They also operate Thousand Islands Fishing Charters, the largest sportfishing charter service on the St. Lawrence River. Having spent the better part of his life on the river, Benas has been featured in numerous magazine and newspaper articles, as well as television programs with regional, national, and international audiences. He is a recognized pioneer of downrigger fishing for muskellunge.

Also from The Countryman Press and Backcountry Guides

Backcountry Fishing Guides
Fishing Vermont's Streams and Lakes
Great Lakes Steelhead: A Guided Tour for Fly Anglers
Best Streams for Great Lakes Steelhead
Trout Streams of Michigan
Mid-Atlantic Trout Streams and Their Hatches
Trout Streams and Hatches of Pennsylvania
Tailwater Trout in the South
Trout Streams of Virginia
Trout Streams of Wisconsin and Minnesota
Good Fishing in the Catskills
Good Fishing in Lake Ontario and Its Tributaries

Other Books About the Region
50 Hikes in the Adirondacks
25 Bicycle Tours in the Adirondacks
25 Mountain Bike Tours in the Adirondacks
50 Hikes in the Lower Hudson Valley
Walks and Rambles in the Western Hudson Valley

We offer many more books on fishing, fly tying, hiking, biking, travel and other subjects. Our books are available at bookstores and outdoor stores nationwide. For more information or a free catalog, please call 1-800-245-4151 or write to us at The Countryman Press, PO Box 748, Woodstock, Vermont 05091. Or you can download our catalog at our web site: www.countrymanpress.com.

LaVergne, TN USA
03 November 2009
162937LV00001B/154/P